Poodle Mistress

*The autobiographical story of
life with nine toy poodles*

SANDI LATIMER

iUniverse, Inc.
Bloomington

Poodle Mistress
The autobiographical story of life with nine toy poodles

iUniverse books may be ordered through booksellers or by contacting:

iUniverse
1663 Liberty Drive
Bloomington, IN 47403
www.iuniverse.com
1-800-Authors (1-800-288-4677)

ISBN: 978-1-4502-8428-8 (pbk)
ISBN: 978-1-4502-8431-8 (ebk)

Printed in the United States of America

iUniverse rev. date: 2/10/2011

To Mom

You always said I would write children's books. I'm saddened that you didn't live long enough to see this story of my "children."

Ollie M. Mosher, November 20, 1916–June 20, 2010

Contents

Meeting My Men

I slowed my blue Buick and shifted into second gear to turn into the trailer park off Route 23, north of Columbus, Ohio. It had been a nearly thirty-mile drive from my apartment in Columbus, and I had had time to think about the type of man who would choose to raise toy poodles. A big, strong man should have an outdoor dog like a German shepherd, a collie, or a lab. A poodle should be wearing a diamond-studded collar and accompany an actress or a ritzy-looking woman dressed in tight fashion pants, high heels, and sunglasses. At least that is what I had pictured. I could not imagine a man raising small dogs. What kind of man was I starting to let into my life?

I drove through the trailer court. Several years earlier, I had worked at the radio station in nearby Delaware and had known people who lived in trailer courts, but I didn't know anyone here until a few weeks ago.

My mind raced back to that night—the Major League All-Star Game of 1973, the only event on the sports calendar. It seemed the quietest summer night at the wire service, United Press International in Columbus, where I rewrote news stories and transmitted them to radio and television clients for their evening newscasts. I was bored. I was performing an exercise of how many ways I could rewrite a news story from the day's happenings. My coworker on the other side of the desk, Jay Gibian, leaned back in his chair and twiddled his thumbs because he had finished his work and couldn't find anything else to do. He hated sports, so that was one less topic we could discuss.

George Thomas, the teletype operator on the other side of the room, was punching tape to transmit stories to newspapers. It was quiet in a sense. The phone wasn't ringing, but the *clickety-clack* of nine teletype machines along the concrete block walls created a noisy rhythm. To have something to do, I picked the phone headset up from the desk,

1

pushed a button to get a dial tone, and placed a routine call to the Ohio Highway Patrol's Communications Center to see if anything was happening in Ohio that would make for at least a one- or two-paragraph news story.

"Hey, you're new there," I said when the phone was answered by a male voice I hadn't heard before. From the sound of his voice, the man on the other end of the line seemed about as busy as I was.

He said that his name was Red and that he flew out of the aviation division, but he was filling in at the communications center because the regular staff was at a coworker's retirement party.

"Gee, they did tell me about that," I said. "I forgot."

We talked for a while, getting to know a little about each other.

"We get off at the same time. Why don't we meet for coffee?" I suggested. Why I was so forward, I still don't know. He refused, telling me that he had to fly the next morning. I didn't think anything more about it.

I was surprised when he called late the next afternoon and asked me out. I had a choice: I could find some place to eat in the middle of the evening—I could take lunch at 7:00 p.m., as usual, or catch something after 11:00 p.m. when my shift ended. Not much was open in downtown Columbus at either hour. I chose to meet him at a little after eleven o'clock at a restaurant-lounge near my apartment.

I wasn't dressed to meet anyone. Working second shift, I always dressed down since only three people worked in the office at that time, and I knew that I wouldn't be sent out on assignment. Not many people stopped in the office after 3:00 p.m.

Most of the people who popped in were delivering news releases that we reporters used to write stories to send to newspapers and radio and television news departments. We had more morning deliveries, because people wanted their stories to go to the afternoon papers; more papers at that time were published in the early afternoon than in the morning. Although we women could wear slacks, I still wasn't comfortable wearing them to work. It was a hot day, and I had chosen a blue sleeveless dress that buttoned down the front, white sandals, and no panty hose. My legs really needed a shave.

In the parking lot of the restaurant-lounge beside a red Ford LTD stood a man with a full head of light red, wavy hair. He was dressed in a shirt, tie, and red sport coat. He was tall. Anyone to me is tall. I stand just shy of five feet, and he towered a good full head above me. His voice had indicated that he was older than my twenty-nine years.

"I'm Sandi," I said as I exited my car that I had parked next to his. "Are you Red? Did you have dinner?"

Since we had both eaten, we chatted over snacks and a drink and listened to the piped-in music. The regular piano player at the lounge played only on weekends, since weeknights didn't create much business.

I soon learned that he was about to celebrate his forty-fifth birthday, had been married twice, and had two adult daughters and two grandchildren. His first marriage ended in divorce and his second in the death of his wife. He lived alone and was raising two toy poodles. One was only three months old and the runt of the litter. That shot my idea that all owners of poodles were women.

Poodles, he told me, are standard, miniature, and toy. Standard are the large ones, fifteen to twenty-two inches high at their shoulders. Miniatures range between ten and fifteen inches, and the toys like he had are ten inches. At the end of the evening, I promised that I'd visit him and meet the dogs.

Focusing my thoughts on finding his place, I reached down for the directions he'd given me. I had no problem finding his mobile home. How many residences have a highway patrol cruiser in front of them? His Ford LTD was parked across the street so that I could park beside the cruiser.

As I climbed the steps to the sliding door on the side of the mobile home, I saw a white poodle and heard it barking on the other side of the door. There was no need to be scared. The little dog didn't look or sound vicious.

Red scooped the dog into his arms and opened the door.

"This must be Jacques Pierre," I said, patting the dog's topknot, the fluffy part that groomers leave on the top of a poodle's head. "And this has to be his son Shane," I said, kneeling to tickle a little white fluff in the middle of the living room. "He's cute."

As I sat on the couch, this fluffy little thing started climbing my leg. Shane spent the rest of the afternoon on my lap or in my arms. I was adopted! I was falling in love with him. Who wouldn't love a puppy not much bigger than my hand?

"Looks like you have a dog," Red said.

While I was fussing over Shane, Jacques hung close to Red. He wasn't sure what to make of me. Jacques and Red had been buddy-buddy for several years, and Jacques hadn't really made friends yet with Shane. They'd only been together a few weeks.

I had fallen for Shane about as quickly as he had fallen for me. I knew that I would have to come back to see him. I didn't want to break anyone's heart, but it wouldn't be fair to come only to see the puppy. Meanwhile, Red was paying attention to me, and I liked it. As we shared a good-bye kiss, I had the feeling that there was more to that kiss. Something told me that I would be back—and not just to see little Shane.

What did I know about poodles? I had had a dog when I was a senior in high school a dozen years or so before. He was a whodunit—a mutt who had his own life and didn't require the high maintenance that poodles do. We were living in a rural area, and it seemed that everyone had dogs. They came with the territory.

Poodles. They are different. I'd always thought that poodles belonged to women and had those haircuts with patches of fur on their rumps, as well as balls of fur around their ankles and the tips of their tails—haircuts that I didn't care for. Poodles were supposed to be prim and proper, weren't they? I didn't know anyone who had poodles, let alone a man!

My feelings for Red grew deeper, and we got together as much as our schedules allowed. We worked different shifts. He was a pilot in the patrol's aviation division, and his hours changed according to the amount of daylight. Generally, I worked four night shifts at UPI—3:00–11:00 p.m. and one overnight shift — 10:00 p.m.–7:00 a.m.

I learned that Red was quite adventuresome and had had the toys to prove it. He had owned a motorcycle since he was old enough to have a driver's license. When he entered the highway patrol academy in December 1951, he taught his fellow classmates how to ride. The patrol began to move from motorcycles to cars. In the 1960s, when the State of Ohio adopted legislation requiring motorcycle riders to get a special endorsement on their operators' licenses, Red taught the driver examiners how to maneuver the designated course. In effect, he was the first person in Ohio to have such an endorsement.

Red also had owned a boat and had done some waterskiing. In 1970, he was one of the many highway patrol officers sent to The Ohio State University to quell unrest during antiwar protests. He used his overtime earnings on flying lessons and purchased an airplane. He had taken his flying lessons from the same person who had given me three lessons not long after I had graduated from college and was working at the radio station in Bucyrus. We both rode bicycles.

It wasn't long before Red and I were making plans to be married. We weren't going to let the fifteen-year age difference stop us.

But my mind kept going back to the poodles. They were nothing like those I had seen in pictures. Those must have been show dogs. These dogs were showing me another side—how they could be friendly and loveable.

These dogs weren't all that prim and proper. They wore leather collars with identification and shot record tags jingling on them, but only when they went outside the fenced-in yard. They were playful. At times, they were close to being human. I felt that they understood what we said.

Shane had already become my dog, but I worried about being accepted by Jacques. He and Red had been together for nearly all of his young life, and it had been the two of them for the past four years—ever since Red's wife had passed away. Almost everywhere Red went, Jacques went. I figured that I could score points if I paid attention to him and fed him.

Red and I became engaged in October, and the following month, Red bought a house in Columbus near my apartment building and moved in Thanksgiving weekend. The house is a bi-level with six rooms that are seven steps up from the front door and two big rooms in the basement that are seven steps down. The first night in the new home, Red worried about how the dogs would act in a strange place. He spread the old jacket he had worn that day on a chair and put the two dogs on it. They curled up together. That was the first time Jacques didn't seem to mind his little protégé being so close. That was also the night the two dogs became friends.

Red and I were married in the spring. Not only did I become a wife, but I also became an instant mother to two dogs.

Jacques Pierre

I am now mother to these two dogs. Or rather Mistress, as I would be known. What did I know about poodles? I was about to learn.

I had grown up in the 1950s in rural Crawford County in north-central Ohio. My father had told me that I was going to college and get set up in a career so that I would be able to support a family if I had to. He always talked about a career, not a job. I followed his advice and chose to pursue journalism. I hadn't given much thought to marriage and a family.

By the time Red and I were married, Jacques Pierre and I were becoming friends.

"He figured that if I accepted you, he had to too," Red said.

But he still had that strong allegiance to his master.

Jacques was now nearly nine, and Shane was almost a year old. They had become the center of our lives. Red had doted on the dogs, but this was all new to me.

Jacques had grown up with Red, and I felt that I might have been intruding into this lifestyle. I worried about how we would get along. They were close, and Jacques was protective of Master. When Red would get gas in the car, Jacques would go with him. At the station, he'd jump on the ledge at the back window and bark at the attendant, following him all around the car. No one was going to mess with Master or Master's car.

When Red would go to work in uniform, out the back door and into his cruiser, Jacques seemed to understand that he was not allowed to go.

The nights when Red would go to work out at the gym at the highway patrol academy were different. He would leave in civilian clothes and go out the front door. That seemed to bother Jacques. He didn't know what to do. He would lie at the top step watching the front door and waiting for Master to return.

Jacques's vigil bothered me at first. I felt a little tense. Had I done something wrong? Didn't he trust me? Did he feel my tension too? Jacques was so accustomed to going with Red that apparently he felt left out. Did he think that he should have gone? All I had to do was look at what they had done. Red had taken him for rides in the bicycle basket, in the car, and in the airplane on a pleasure flight. Even when he went to a restaurant, he'd bring home a doggie bag with goodies that actually went to the dog.

About a month after Red moved into the house, a new family moved into the house immediately south of it. They had a dog, George, and five little girls, including two sets of twins. George was a black dog with short hair, and he looked like he was part beagle and part terrier. As we became acquainted with our new neighbors, so did the dogs, especially Jacques and George.

Jacques had seniority, and he let George know it. I don't think George and Jacques liked each other much. Jacques would gnaw at the chain-link fence that separated the two yards. George would bark back. Our yard was a little higher and had a concrete walkway alongside the fence. That's a strange place for a sidewalk. George made a path on his side by running up and down the fence. I'm glad they never got together in an open field.

A year or so later, we noticed Jacques's eyes clouding over, and he bumped into things. Our vet told us that poodles are susceptible to cataracts. That was what affected Jacques. We decided that his age was against him; he was too old for surgery. Our vet told us not to move furniture.

Jacques knew where everything was, and we didn't want to disrupt his life. I felt sorry for the little fella, but he continued to go about everyday life with seemingly little trouble.

Occasionally, he bumped into something, stepped back, and walked around it. He learned to feel his way around. He would reach out with a paw to find the first step. Sometimes, he would lose count of the steps and try to jump an imaginary one at the top. We'd try not to laugh.

We noticed—as happens in humans—that when one of the senses goes, another becomes stronger. One evening, when I put the dinner plates on the table, Jacques went to where Red was sitting in the recliner reading the paper, and he barked. That was his way of telling him that dinner was ready. Every time I put the dinner plates on the table, Jacques would seek Red out.

I started testing him. I put salad plates, bowls, or cups and saucers on the table. No response. Red got into the game. He would hide. He went into the bathroom and closed the door. I put dinner plates on the table. Jacques would go to the bathroom door, bark, whine, and scratch the door. Red would quietly go down in the basement to his work corner. I put dinner plates on the table. Jacques would go find Master.

Why was Jacques doing this? He didn't seek out Red for dinner before his eyesight failed.

"He wants to make sure that he gets the plate to lick after dinner," Red guessed.

One evening, the woman across the street was coming over for dinner. I made the mistake of setting the table early. When the dinner plates went on the table, Jacques went in search of Red and started barking. He wouldn't quit until Red went to the table and sat in the chair as if he were eating. He had to sit at the table until the neighbor woman arrived.

I dropped down on my hands and knees and gave him a big hug.

"You did great," I said.

How many times I did that. I wanted to let him know that I was his friend, that I wanted to help him, and that I loved him. He tolerated me, but I knew that he always loved Master more.

Acquiring Zeke

Not long after we were married, Judy Bender, a poodle owner in Marion, called Red to see if Jacques Pierre was still available for stud service.

Jacques had a long line of offspring. Red generally would take payment rather than pick of the litter—except the last time when he acquired Shane. Often, as he used a particular item, he would say, "Jacques bought this." That's how he purchased the set of leathers he wore when he rode the motorcycle.

"Yes, Jacques is still available," he told Judy. She wasn't sure when her female, Christy, would be ready, but she wanted to have a respected male lined up when the time came. She said that she could sell several pups. It wasn't until fall that she called back to set up a time for the two dogs to get together.

Red and I were concerned about this date. Jacques was getting up in years. We wondered if he would still be good.

Usually, people figure that one year in a human's life is equal to seven years in a dog's life. But we learned through our vet that a dog's life to human years is figured a little differently. The first year is equal to sixteen human years, or an age at which the dog can reproduce. The next year is equal to eight years, and then every subsequent year is equal to four years. By this time, Jacques was nine and a half, or, in human years, fifty-four years old. He should still be able to perform successfully.

Judy brought Christy to us. Females in season give off an odor that arouses the male. Christy hardly had time to realize where she was when Jacques realized what his job was. Now we had to wait six weeks to see the results—if there were any.

Around the middle of December, we got a call from Judy. Christy had four pups December 10. Jacques was still good! However, Red and Judy hadn't settled on payment.

"She might have been able to sell a dozen pups last summer," I said. "But look at the timing. It's two weeks before Christmas, and those pups won't be able to go until the end of January."

"She'll sell them, all right," said my husband, the eternal optimist. "She has a good reputation."

"But it's Christmas," I contended. "Money is tight. And in late January, people are getting their credit card bills. They won't have the money."

Christmas came. So did New Year's. One evening at work, I had a phone call from Red.

"That's what you wanted all of the time, isn't it?" I asked him before I hung up the phone, shook my head, and returned to the task of rewriting news stories for the broadcast report.

I had the next night off, so when Red came home from work, we drove the forty miles to Marion, where Red had once lived, to look at the puppies—four cuddly white toy poodle puppies in a playpen.

Red fell in love with a little male with a black belly. It was the only one with a belly darker than normal. That little puppy came to Columbus that night in Red's coat pocket.

He was only five weeks and a couple of days old. The pups were getting teeth, and Mama wouldn't be letting them feed from her much longer. My prediction had come true. All of those who had wanted pups last summer were nowhere to be found by December. The woman who once said that she could sell six was lucky to be able to sell two. Instead of taking stud fees, Red took pick of the litter.

I knew that he had wanted another dog. Jacques was aging and wouldn't be around for too many more years. Shane was definitely my dog; he didn't want a thing to do with Red unless he wanted something. Red would need a dog.

Our new puppy, now nameless, spent his first night in his new home in a yellow plastic clothes basket beside the register in the front room. The next day, Red went shopping at a drugstore a block away and came home with a white stuffed elephant.

"I couldn't find a white dog as a substitute mother," he said. The puppy accepted the elephant. The two were alike; neither had a name. They were about the same size too.

After several days of calling our new puppy every name we could think of, we settled on Zeke, short for Ezekiel Jacques Pierre. Ezekiel seemed to come from out of the blue, but the Jacques Pierre came from his father's name. The pup now had a name, but the little elephant never did.

Zeke had big feet. It seemed his feet grew, and then as he grew, his feet continued to grow. I often called him Big Foot.

The elephant was Zeke's buddy. Jacques and Shane never played with it. Zeke shook it, threw it, chased it, cuddled up with it, and chewed on it. As the elephant's eyes loosened, I tried sewing them on tighter. Zeke was still hard on it.

Reluctantly, and for safety's sake, I cut off the eyes and used an old T-shirt to sew patches over the eye slots. That didn't make any difference to Zeke. He still played with the elephant until he was a little more than a year old. One day, he thought it was a female. It was funny, but embarrassing. I wondered if he would take after his father and be used for stud service. By this time, the elephant was about the color of a real elephant, a dirty gray. It looked shabby, so we took it away.

We couldn't throw it out, so the elephant was tossed onto a shelf in a back room closet. Surprisingly, Zeke didn't miss his friend and didn't go looking for it.

To this day, when I come across that elephant, I have to wipe away a flood of memories that flow down my cheeks. Even Red will get choked up with the mention of the elephant.

That Darn Zeke

Growing up, Zeke had an ornery streak. Or was it just his being a puppy? Shane hadn't acted that way when he was little. He was too cute and was made a fuss over. Zeke was different. He did a lot of things that were out of the ordinary—or at least I thought they were. At times, I could liken him to a child.

Early in the spring, Red's shift with the patrol began to fluctuate. It seemed like an unusual schedule, but we saw it as normal. The patrol worked to keep planes in the air throughout daylight hours. In winter, all of the pilots worked the same shift, since daylight was in short supply. But as days lengthened, some pilots went in early and worked their eight hours, while others started their eight-hour shifts later in the day. At this time, Red was working three late shifts, followed by two early shifts, and then he had two days off. Getting off in midafternoon and not returning to work until a late shift two days later almost became three days off.

My schedule was about as erratic. I generally worked weekends, which gave me days off in the middle of the week. Once in a great while, our two days off coincided; generally, they did not. Working as a reporter for a wire service, a business that operated around the clock, what people thought of as an unusual schedule was the norm for us. We both took our unusual schedules as part of life.

One particular day, Red was working a late shift and would go in early the next morning. He would eat dinner and try to get some sleep—or at least some rest—so that he'd be fresh and alert to fly the next morning.

That afternoon, I had seen a beautiful red tulip in the backyard flower bed in front of the evergreen trees. From the porch, it looked like a radish on a vegetable tray at dinner—red tipped with white.

"I must tell Red about it when he gets home," I said and went about my work. He likes tulips, and I had planted several in that flower bed the previous fall.

"You have to see this one tulip," I said excitedly when Red came home.

"I can't get a good look at it now," he said. "It's too dark. I'll check on it when I get home tomorrow afternoon."

When he worked a late shift like this, daylight was nearly gone when he came home from the airport on the northwest corner of the city. We lived on the far west side. Red liked a lot of daylight to view the flowers.

"Don't forget about the tulip," I reminded him before he left for work the next morning.

"I won't," he said.

The next morning, the tulip still looked good. It had held its form and still looked like that adorning radish. I could hardly wait until Red came home so that he could see it.

I kept an eye on the dogs when I let them outside. The neighbors behind us had a big English sheepdog, and I didn't know how friendly it could be if it jumped the fence. With all of that hair over its eyes, how well could it see? It was a lot bigger than my little poodles. Shane, the runt of the litter, didn't grow much. It wasn't long before Zeke had outgrown him. That English sheepdog's foot was probably about the size of Shane. I had to keep an eye on all of the dogs when they were in the backyard.

Red came home in the middle of the afternoon. The dogs were excited and followed him around. I was starting to get dinner. Within minutes, Red appeared in the kitchen and asked, "Now where is that tulip you wanted me to look at?"

I turned around, looked up at him, and tried not to show my lower lip that I knew had to be quivering.

"Zeke ate it," I said, almost in tears.

I had been sitting on the top step just out the back door watching the dogs play in the yard. Zeke had walked over to that one little white-tipped red tulip and bit it off. I didn't even have time to yell at him to stop. None of the other dogs had ever done anything like that before, and none of them did anything like that later. If he was going to attack a flower, why did he have to target the one I'd had my eye on?

That wasn't the only time the dogs got into the flower bed. One day, not long after that episode, I thought Murphy's Law was kicking in. "If anything can go wrong, it will." I had to go to a noon luncheon/news conference and then write the story before I started my broadcast-writing shift in midafternoon. I had put the dogs outside while I was getting dressed. I was about ready to leave.

I opened the back door to let the dogs in. Then I saw them. No way were they getting in. I had to carefully pick each one up and carry him back to the bathroom and spray the mud off his legs, towel dry him, and brush him. Repeat that two times. They had decided to take a run through the flower bed made muddy by an early morning rain.

I never could tell which one led the dirty deed; of course, they weren't going to tell.

The incident that embarrassed us all happened on Zeke's first Christmas as a member of our family. We had taken all three dogs with us when we went to Bucyrus, seventy miles to the north, to visit with my family. The dogs were well behaved in the car, and my stepdad, Bill, enjoyed spending time with them.

After getting dinner plans taken care of and the meat in the oven, Mom and I decided to visit a friend. We took Shane with us. My brother Jim and his friend Dean wanted to visit a couple of their friends, and they asked Red to go along. He took Zeke. That left Jacques at home with my stepdad.

Mom and I returned home first. Jacques had to sniff all around Shane. I wondered if he'd smelled the scent from the dog where we had visited.

About a half an hour later, the guys came home. Jim and Dean were laughing hard when they came through the door. Red was carrying Zeke, and Red's face was redder than his hair. We had a hard time getting anything from them. Jim and Dean were laughing hard, and Red kept saying, "I was embarrassed." Zeke was on the floor by this time, and the other two had to sniff him out.

It took a few minutes for the guys to compose themselves. Red finally explained that the people they went to visit had a white cat, "and Zeke tried to mount it." Jim and Dean broke out laughing again.

That was another indication of what might transpire. It also led us to start thinking whether he would be a good stud like his father, even though he showed just one testicle.

Jacques Pierre, Zeke, and Shane in the winter of 1976

Zeke

Zeke's puppy stage lasted a long time—or maybe it seemed that way since he was the first dog that I had seen grow up from almost a newborn. Could we have helped exaggerate that orneriness because we babied him?

One thing he learned early was to pray. Red would hold him like he was holding a child, and Zeke would bring his front paws together.

"See Zeke pray," Red would say.

"He's praying that you don't drop him," I quipped.

Zeke was good at sitting up too. He had a long tail; not much had been cut off when he was a few days old. Most poodles have just a little stub, but not Zeke. I often thought that he balanced himself on that tail. He wouldn't sit on command—only at mealtime and then only beside Master's chair.

Zeke was primarily Red's dog, but he liked me too. He also protected me—in a way.

About once a year, Red would have to attend a day of training—something routine for highway patrol officers. Those refresher sessions dealt with such topics as weapon safety and marksmanship, personal safety, and riot training. After a day of training, he'd show me what he had gone through. He'd ask me to attack him, and he'd fend me off. It was not unusual for me to end up on the floor. I'm not the most graceful person, and I am not an actress or a stuntwoman. I was awkward at trying to do what Red wanted me to do. My ending up on the floor didn't sit that well with Zeke. Apparently, he thought that Master was hurting Mistress. After that, all Red had to do was make a fist and pretend that he was going to hit me. Zeke would growl at him. That surprised Red. Wow! I had protection—albeit from a dog who weighed less than ten pounds.

Poodles are supposed to be intelligent dogs, and at times, our dogs exhibited that intelligence. The night *Old Yeller* was on television, Red watched it from the recliner, and I watched from the couch on the other side of the living room. Zeke was stretched out in front of the television. He got up periodically and went into the kitchen for a bite of dog food and a drink of water. I started checking when he left the room. I got Red's attention, and we both watched him. Zeke left during commercials and then returned to his stretched-out position facing the television to continue watching the show.

Zeke understood a lot of other things too. The winter that he was two, we were in an energy crisis. Streetlights remained off at dusk in an effort to conserve energy. That made it difficult for me, since I worked in downtown Columbus at night. I would park my car on a street with no parking meters and walk three blocks to the office. That was in the middle of the afternoon. I'd move my car close to the building at six o'clock when the parking meters were free. The security guard in our building carried a flashlight when he walked me to my car when I got off around midnight. Schools were even closed for several weeks—another attempt to conserve energy.

Only a few weeks earlier, Zeke had learned that he could go to the window in the mornings and watch children walk to the nearby school. He seemed to understand that Monday through Friday were school days, because he wouldn't go to the window on Saturdays or Sundays. If he did, I didn't know it, because I worked a third shift on weekends and was in bed at that time. Then came the day when the schools closed for a few weeks, and he didn't have any children to watch. He'd come over and look at me dejectedly as if to ask, "Where are the kids?"

"Zeke, we don't have school for a while," I'd tell him. I'd get on the floor, look him in the eye, and try to explain what was going on. Back and forth between the window and me he went. He must have forgotten that routine, because he never did go back to the window when the kids went back to school.

Besides the window, he had a couple of places to hang out. The living/dining area of the house is one long room. Under that ceiling-to-floor window is a hot-air register. At the dining room end is a café-style window that comes down almost to the top of the chairs around the dining table. A hot-air register sits under that window. A third such register sits along the wall near the entrance to the kitchen.

Shane would often lie on the register near the kitchen, and the hot air would make his ears flap like wings on a bird. When the air became too hot for Shane, he'd abandon the register, and Zeke would take over. It wasn't long until Zeke wised up to what was happening. As soon as the furnace clicked on, he would head to the register, lie down, and stare between the slats, looking for the hot air.

He also liked a little chair that I'd had since I was six. It sat in the corner of the living room and soon became his favorite spot. He'd curl up on it and sleep—or he'd sit up tall as if he were asserting his authority.

The summer that I was five, our house was destroyed by fire. We were trying to re-establish our lives a couple of months later when I turned six. My family was at a furniture store when I fell for this chair—a miniature of an adult one and just right for a child my size. I begged Daddy to buy it for me for my birthday. The salesman threw it in with our purchases that day. Zeke was just a little tyke when he discovered that he could climb onto that chair. When no one reprimanded him, he took it over, letting everyone know that it was his. One day, Red's brother and sister-in-law Horace and Zelma were visiting from West Lafayette in eastern Ohio, one hundred miles away. Horace put his hat on the chair. Zeke sat in front of the chair and stared at it longingly. He knew that he shouldn't get up on the hat. Red finally asked his brother to move his hat. When Horace moved his hat, Zeke climbed onto the chair, turned around, sat down, and faced everyone.

Jacques sat on Red's lap that afternoon, and Shane sat on mine. I don't think they knew what to make of our company.

Red always considered Jacques a model dog. Perhaps it was because it was his first dog in adulthood.

"I could leave him in the car with a bag of doughnuts, and he wouldn't touch them," he'd say.

Try that with another dog—or me!

We could be gone for several hours and not worry about any damage to the house. The dogs knew enough to do their business in the basement on the concrete floor where it was easy to clean.

Red had cut a small square in the basement door so that the dogs could go up and downstairs at will. It made a lot of sense to have a hole in the door instead of leaving the door wide open. We could slide a piece of paneling over the hole when necessary. The dogs had their choice of eating and sleeping in the basement or coming upstairs and sitting on the front windowsill to absorb the morning sunshine and watch what was going on outside—one advantage of that ceiling-to-floor window.

We had no qualms about taking off for homecoming at Kent State, my alma mater, one nice fall day when we engineered a Saturday off together. I worked on sports on weekends, and it was unusual for me to have a weekend off in the fall and winter.

One of the last things we did before we left that day was to pull one of the cushions off the couch in the living room to make it easier for them to jump up onto it throughout the day. Jacques, Shane, and Zeke had plenty of food and water, their toys, and one another.

It was a three-hour drive to Kent, followed by lunch, a football game, and three-hour drive back. Late in the evening when we returned, we knew that we would have a mess in the basement to clean up, but we didn't expect a mess in the living room. It was a different kind of mess. One of the three had gotten into the wastebasket and found a bit of breakfast garbage. Broken eggshells and tea from torn tea bags were strewn around the living room floor and on the couch. Even the *Hustler* magazine I had bought out of curiosity when photos of a topless Jackie Onassis were published was chewed—but only the pages with Jackie's photos.

"I was certain that magazine was in the rack when we left," I said.

Was someone mad because we left without him? Would Jacques really do something like that? Shane was too small to get into the wastebasket. Zeke was still in the puppy stage and already bigger than Shane. And the wastebasket hadn't been tipped over.

About a year or so later, Red and I had an afternoon free and decided to go flying. I had purchased an airplane in 1976. The state received federal funds because Ohio cut the speed limit and instituted other practices during that recent energy crisis. This money was used to purchase new planes for the highway patrol. The planes they had been flying were renumbered and put up for sale. I bought one.

Red had logged about four thousand hours as a pilot, and I had only a few hours with an instructor. We enjoyed having the plane, but we encountered some limitations. We could only fly during the day, because Red did not have an instrument rating. When we did fly, we were limited where we could go because of a lack of ground transportation. We bought folding bicycles, but generally airports are on the outskirts of town. These bicycles had small wheels, and it looked like we had commandeered children's bikes. We pedaled forever and got nowhere. We tried to land at an airport where a restaurant was on site.

We had chosen to fly that day into an airport that had a restaurant. When we returned home, we walked in the back door, through the kitchen, and into the dining/living room to find on the living room floor the remains of a loaf of bread that I had taken out of the freezer before we left.

"I'm sure that I put it as far back on the counter as possible," I said, surveying the floor littered with chunks of bread and shreds of the plastic wrapper. "Who's the culprit?" I asked as I watched the dogs head down the back steps and out into the backyard. I knew that I wouldn't get a reply.

Red and I were on our hands and knees picking up bread and plastic bag pieces before getting the sweeper out to clean up the crumbs.

"Jacques would never do this," he maintained.

His age was against him; he was more than ten years old. Shane was too small to jump that high. Or was he? Did Zeke do it? Did all three get into the bread? Or did one?

I leaned back and sat in the middle of the floor, laughed, and said, "I sure would have liked to have had a camera in place—not to catch the culprit as much as to see how he did it."

"Whoever did it had to get up on the wastebasket," Red said.

The wastebasket—with a lid on it—sat in front of the broom closet door next to the counter.

The culprit had to get up on the wastebasket to jump up on the counter, walk over the front edge of the range, tightrope walk across the sink, turn the corner to the counter where the bread was up against the splashboard, drag it to the edge, push it off, jump down, and haul it to the living room.

Having three dogs was much like having children, I guess. They were fine alone, but put them together and we never knew what they would do.

I could suddenly hear my mother's words about my neighbor girl Judy and me. She would say that we were good alone, but oh, the trouble we got into together—like pouring hot water down the hill one winter day to make it icier for our sled riding. That was the hill I had to go up and down to get drinking water from their pump. Mom made me carry a bucket of water home that night—down that slippery hill and not on the road.

Mom could punish me, but I couldn't punish a dog. I couldn't make him pay for what he had done. I couldn't spank him because he wouldn't know what I was hitting him for. He'd probably think that I was abusing him.

What was I to do? Just stew about it? They weren't going to squeal on one another.

After we cleaned up the mess, the wastebasket found a new home—inside the broom closet.

Love Goes Both Ways

After three years of catering to dogs, I was accustomed to having them underfoot. I learned to carry food from the oven to the table in the dining area five steps away without my feet tangling with dogs' feet or dropping a hot casserole dish. I learned how to share a bed with more than another human being. I often wondered what their dog bed was for. They were definitely a strong part of the family, and I referred to them as "kids."

As we got older, changes occurred in our lives. On our second anniversary in 1976, Red surprised me—and I think himself—by suddenly retiring from the highway patrol. He hadn't been feeling well. He had had a head cold, and it hampered his flying. Instead of working in the aviation division, he was sent to the communications center. The constant ringing of phones and all of the other noises bothered him. Without seriously thinking, he figured that he had the years and could buy his eighteen months of military time and have a decent retirement.

I came home from the hairdresser that afternoon and was greeted with, "I retired." I wasn't ready for that, and I don't think that he was either. When he was unable to rescind his hastily made decision, he went looking for another job. He had experience in enforcement and in security. He had begun to worry about the growing number of people on the streets carrying weapons and decided that he didn't want to continue in enforcement. He went looking for security jobs. One place wouldn't even talk with him because he didn't have a college education. But when he interviewed with BankOhio, it was a different story.

"Go get fitted for a uniform," he was told when he talked about his twenty-five years experience with the highway patrol.

In June of 1976 at the age of nearly forty-nine, he began his second career—this one in security with a bank that was opening a new office in downtown Columbus. Getting in at the beginning of this operation, he was able to help mold the security force and guidelines.

Jacques at this time was twelve years old, or, as our vet would figure it, sixty-four years old. Either way one looked at it, he was getting old for a little poodle.

By 1977, Jacques's age began to show. In September of that year, he began having difficulty climbing the stairs to come inside. We'd carry him in, cuddling him and letting him know that it was all right; we understood his difficulty, his aging.

Did he, or any dog, understand such things? Were they aware of changes in their bodies? Who knows what goes through their little minds? They can't communicate in words—only by their actions. Often a lick on the face—a kiss, if you will—says a lot.

One night, when we brought Jacques up the back stairs, he was so weak that he could hardly stand when we tried to put him on the floor. Red sat on the foot of the bed and held him.

"He's dying," he said soberly, almost in tears.

I got down on my knees to be at Jacques's level. I petted him and tried not to let him see or hear my feelings. "I love you, Jacques. Breathe good for Mistress."

"It's no use. He's gone," Red said. "He knew you loved him."

"Look! He's moving. He's not gone," I said.

"That's just the reaction to death," Red said.

Tears flowed from both of us. Red carried the lifeless body downstairs. I tried to keep Shane and Zeke with me, but I couldn't. Those little ones were far too strong for me at that moment. They broke away from me and followed Red to see what he was going to do with their father's body.

Red shed more tears than he had a year earlier when his brother and sister passed away a couple months apart. I wasn't the pillar of strength that I had been when he lost them. We hugged each other and let the tears flow. I hadn't experienced the death of someone so close since my father died seventeen years earlier when I was sixteen.

The next morning, after Red went to work, I slipped over to the florist about a mile away and bought thirteen yellow roses tied in a yellow ribbon with Jacques's name on it. Thirteen—one for each year of his life—and yellow because it means love. I left the vase of flowers on the dining room table and went to work. It was hard trying to concentrate and act as though nothing was wrong.

"You didn't have to spend all of that money on just a dog," Red said sternly when I walked in the door that night.

"He wasn't just a dog," I countered. "He was part of our family."

I was hurt. I felt that Jacques was as much mine as his.

The other two dogs—Shane and Zeke, sons of Jacques from his last two litters—sensed the loss and weren't quite as spirited as usual. Shane even tried to crawl into the plastic bag where Red had put Jacques's body the night before.

The sun was slipping below the horizon when we held an improvised funeral service at the little grave Red had dug. We made one last good-bye pat on our friend's side, wiped our tears, and placed Jacques in the grave. Tears flowed again as we shoveled dirt over him.

The next day, I felt a little better, but I was still a little miffed about Red's initial reaction to the flowers. Apparently, a night's sleep had helped him too.

He hugged me and said, "Those flowers were a nice gesture. It meant a lot to me."

The flowers soon died. I saved the yellow ribbon and taped it on a photo hanging on the wall—one that I had taken of all three dogs on the couch.

Shane Andre II

To my bubby—a special word to describe my baby and my buddy.

You're so small, but your curiosity is so large. Your eyes are on me so much of the time, watching everything I do. When I walk from room to room, you're right with me, so close that I have to watch that I don't step on you.

I close you out of the bathroom, but you knock until I let you in. You are fascinated by water swirling in the toilet when it flushes.

When I sit in a chair, you climb on my lap, watching me sew, eat, read, peel apples, or even type. I have a hard time getting comfortable in the leather reclining swivel chair, because you think that's your chair.

You don't think much of my husband. You don't remember that he named you and bottle-fed you when you were a baby. You'll try to get close to him, reaching up to shake his hand. When he extends his hand, you make such mean sounds. But you'll readily accept anyone else's hand. When my husband tries to cut your hair, you squirm so much that he is afraid he'll cut you, and it takes so long for him to give you a decent cut.

You're not much for going outside to play. I put you out, but in a couple of minutes, you want inside.

At breakfast, you climb on my lap and stare longingly at whoever is eating toast. You thoroughly chew what little pieces of toast you get. It's your favorite food. You also persuade me to give you pieces of carrots, apples, and potatoes as I peel them. Really, you're a good eater, cleaning up everything I put in front of you.

You understand English so well, and you dance to your favorite words. You try so hard to climb into the bicycle basket by yourself, but it's a long, hard climb, and I have to put you in for our bicycle ride.

You're the first one out the front door when I go for the mail. You know where I'm going even when I pick up an envelope. You like to run up and down along the hedge in the front yard.

You can sit for hours at the bay window in the living room, communicating with passersby. That window also provides you with a firsthand view of anyone coming to the house. If the visitor is a stranger, you are the first to let me know and the first to make sure that no harm comes to me.

You have toys to play with and also your big little brother, but you want me to play with you. You kiss me when I hug and kiss you and tell you that I love you.

If I spread the newspaper on the floor to read it, you sit on it and reach up to kiss me.

You're the head of the welcoming committee when I come home from work, regardless of the hour.

Although you take several naps during the day, I have no trouble getting you to bed at night. All I have to say is "Are you ready for bed?" and you grab a toy and run for the bed so fast that it looks like a streak of white lightning. Sometimes all I have to do is turn off the TV set or lamp or just take a step toward the bedroom. By the time I get there, you're waiting for me.

But somehow, Shane, as your seventh birthday approaches, I still don't have the heart to tell you that you're my three-and-one-half-pound poodle.

This writing in 1980 was an assignment for a creative writing class I took through the Creative Activities Program at The Ohio State University.

Two other older women were in the class with me, along with a half a dozen more traditional college-age students. This wasn't a for-credit class; it was just a six-week fun class that we paid to attend.

The assignment had been to write a description of a character. The following week, the younger people were eager to read their work. They struggled to describe a human character they would put in a book. We three older women were the last to read. I can't remember what one woman wrote, but I do remember that it was cleverly done. The other woman described her son, a marine, as if he were being auctioned as a slave. It also was cleverly written. I was the last to read.

Having been a journalist since the age of thirteen, I could easily write journalism-style news stories, features, and broadcast reports. Much of it was a repeat of what someone had told me.

Creative writing was new to me, and I was having trouble lightening up. I was good at writing within space constraints and at repeating what others had said, but I struggled for creativity.

I'd tried creative writing before, but my work seemed too stiff. Then came this assignment. The words seemed to jump onto the page. I had read the item so much that I almost knew it from memory. As I read that night in class, I glanced around the room at the other students. One young man was listening intently. He gripped the edge of the table. When I reached the last sentence, he dropped his head on the table and grumbled, "And she was describing a dog!"

"It was effective, wasn't it?" the instructor asked him.

That comment, although not directed at me, meant a lot.

The topic was easy. In writing, you should write what you know. I really knew this little fella, the one who climbed up my leg and stayed on my lap the day I met him.

Shane was one of two pups in Jacques's next-to-last litter. He was the runt of the litter and had to be bottle-fed. Red thought that Shane wouldn't make it and often prided his own efforts at keeping him alive. The pup had been promised to someone who lived in an apartment. Since Red had helped feed him at infancy, he couldn't stand to see him go to anyone else. He took pick of the litter instead of stud fees.

Shane hadn't been living with Red and Jacques any more than a few weeks when I showed up. That pup grew to like me—and only me.

"I'm the one who saved him, fed him, gave him a home, and he growls at me," Red often said. I think that Shane had been given the wrong name. He should have been called White Shadow, because he tagged along behind me much of the time.

Red chose the name Shane from one of his favorite movies, Alan Ladd's *Shane*. Toward the end of the movie, as Ladd's character Shane was walking away from the ranch house, little Brandon deWilde ran after him, calling, "Shane! Come back, Shane! Mother needs you!" That was one phrase I never had to use. Shane didn't get too far from me.

One day, when Red came home from work, I was sitting on a step stool at the sink peeling apples to make applesauce. Jacques had met him at the door.

"Where's Shane?" he asked.

I pointed to my lap. There, curled up in my lap, lay Shane as I peeled away. Shane looked up. "Grrr," he growled, and Red pulled back.

He liked other people, though. He acted as if he were a bodyguard when my friend Jean visited with her infant daughter. Laura was small enough that she could be left on the couch as we chatted and drank coffee a few feet away. Shane jumped up on the couch and sat beside her, watching her intently. He never tried to lick her face or touch her in any way. He was her protector.

I had a good laugh the day I took him with me to visit Jean. Laura was old enough to string a few words together. Jean had a cat that wanted nothing to do with Shane. The cat knew that he was a dog and that the two species didn't get along.

The cat kept climbing higher with each step Shane took, although he didn't even acknowledge the cat. I don't think he knew what a cat was. This may have been the first time that he had seen one.

Laura would laugh and clap her little hands. Laura hadn't been around dogs, either, and all she knew was "Kitty." She would reach out to pet him and say, "Kitty." We spent the afternoon trying to get her to say "Doggie" or even "Shane," but without success.

Since Shane liked me so well, I wondered if he would like to go bicycle riding. One day, I put him in the plastic, wicker-style basket on my bike and pushed it around the basement. He loved it! He sat in the basket and hardly moved. I may have even detected a little smile on that face. We used a big brass snap to hook one end to his collar and the other end to the basket so that he couldn't get out. I don't think I ever needed it, but I used it all of the time for safety's sake.

We would ride around the block or through the neighborhood. One day, we rode down the street to a Dairy Queen-type store where I bought an ice cream cone. A woman came up to me and wanted to make a fuss over Shane. As we were talking, I would take an occasional lick on my ice cream so that it didn't drip. When the woman laughed, I realized that Shane was licking off the other side.

Sometimes, I think Shane understood more than I gave him credit for—like the day I had books to take back to the library and was planning to ride the bike. I couldn't take him, because dogs weren't allowed in public buildings, and I wasn't going to leave him outside with the bike. By this time, Shane wanted to go everywhere with me. If I mentioned the bike, he shot down the steps to the basement where I kept the bike. This time, I spelled it out, saying, "B-i-k-e."

"What was that?" Red asked as a white streak raced past him.

That was Shane running down to the basement. By the time I got there, he was trying to climb up the wheel to get into the basket. I had a dog that could spell! I had to push him around the basement for a while before I left.

Not only did we have regular street bicycles, but we also had folding bicycles with added motors and Red's Exercycle that I said had a serial number of 1. It had four legs and could be powered by pedal or two speeds by electricity. The handlebars could be rotated to provide for different types of workouts. The seat reminded me of one on an old tractor. Red often rode that Exercycle while he watched television.

Depending on the amount of work at the office or the type of work that was needed, my shifts varied. A few times, I worked a shift from 1:00 to 9:00 p.m. One night, when I arrived home around 9:30, no welcoming committee met me at the front door. I could hear the TV in the basement. I left my purse and keys on the steps going up to the living room and went down into the basement. I wish I'd had a camera.

Red had removed the basket from my bicycle and strapped it on the handlebars of the Exercycle. In it sat Shane, looking completely content as the handlebars went up and down as Red pedaled and watched TV.

He let Red do something for him that night, because it was something that he wanted to do.

Shane would bark occasionally, mostly when the letter carrier approached the mailbox. He once barked at a woman weeding her flower bed while we were riding the bike. But mostly he howled like a coyote, and he assumed the position of a howling coyote. He'd sit atop the back of the couch, stretch his neck, raise his head, and let out an ear-piercing howl.

That dog sure did have an unusual personality, but we both loved him.

Star

In the fall of 1981, Red and I were at a party and hovering around a bonfire trying to keep warm. I was standing a few people away from Red when I heard him say, "I'd like to get a motor home."

On the way home, I asked, "What's a motor home?"

During the next few months, we occasionally checked the classified ads in the paper. The following spring, Red found a motor home at a car dealer, and we made an appointment to look at it. It had been used for tailgating at football games and hardly showed any wear. The salesman handed me the keys and said, "Let's go for a ride."

I'd never driven anything that large before. It was a Sprinter model—twenty-seven feet from bumper to bumper. The huge steering wheel was almost horizontal, whereas the steering wheel in a car is closer to vertical. Surprisingly, I felt comfortable driving.

On the way home, Red and I talked over our finances. I had a certificate of deposit coming due in a few days, and I'd put the airplane up for sale. That was my half if he could match it.

We'd had the airplane since 1976. It was nice to say that we had one, but we were limited in using it. The weather had to be good, and we had to have ground transportation. That's where we thought our folding bikes would come in handy. Those twenty-inch wheels just hadn't cut it. We adults were accustomed to twenty-six-inch wheels.

Only a few places dotted our aviation map where we could fly and not need ground transportation. Not many airports had restaurants. A few times, we would just fly out somewhere for a meal—to Urbana or New Philadelphia—or to try to help me learn to land, which I never accomplished. I'd get the plane down close to the ground, but suddenly, I'd pull up, and Red had to take over and land.

The possibilities were greater with a motor home. Drive it. Park it.

Live in it. Eat in it. The dogs loved it. Oh, yes, they allowed us in. After all, they had to have someone drive it, park it, and feed them.

That first summer, we crisscrossed Ohio in our motor home, getting accustomed to a new lifestyle. My schedule that summer coincided with Red's. Jacques was gone by that time, Shane was nine, and Zeke was seven. We camped at state parks and sometimes spent a night in a roadside rest area when we couldn't find a place to camp. We were learning firsthand how popular camping is.

In August, Shane developed a respiratory problem. He coughed for a couple of days. I spent a lot of time with him, holding him and massaging his throat. On the second day of coughing, I took him to our vet, who told me that the respiratory problem Shane endured was not unusual in poodles and that it could not be treated. I petted Shane as he lay on the examining table. "I love you," I said. The vet assured me that that dog knew that he was much loved.

Then he inserted a needle into Shane's neck. I thought he was giving him some medication that would help him. The vet explained what he was doing. I wanted him to stop. I wanted Shane in my arms again. It was too late. Shane's little heart stopped beating. He was gone.

I didn't know what to do. The vet found a towel to wrap around Shane. I had to be in shock. He put my dog's body in a box and led me out a side door so that I wouldn't have to pass through the waiting room filled with other people and their pets.

He helped me put the box in the trunk of the car. I felt awful about leaving Shane alone in the trunk. He didn't belong there. He belonged in the front seat with me, wrapped around my neck like a white fur collar. He really didn't know where he was. The last thing he heard (and I hope he understood) was "I love you."

We were still seeing a vet in Marion, about an hour's drive away. I cried much of the way to Columbus. I stopped at the bank where Red was working. I cried as I told him about Shane's last minutes—how I petted him and had told him that he was loved. My husband put his arms around me and held me tightly.

"I'm getting you a female dog for your birthday," he said.

A few days later, it dawned on me that getting a female dog was Red's plan for a long time. He was nearly forty-six when we were married. He'd said that he didn't want children at such a late stage in his life, because he didn't want to go to their graduations in a wheelchair. He'd often spoken of raising a litter of pups. Instead of two-legged children, we were planning to become parents to more four-legged ones.

My birthday was several weeks away. Meanwhile, we were down to one dog, Zeke.

Although Zeke seemed to favor my husband, I think he realized that I was alone and spent much time with me. I needed that. I think he sensed my loss and wanted to console me.

Red and I started talking about the new dog. When he told me that he was getting the female, he didn't even know for sure that the mother dog was pregnant.

"What if she doesn't have a female?" he asked one day. "Would you settle for a male?"

"Yes," I said. I was lost without a dog; it was the first time in nine years that I hadn't had one. Something was missing in my life. I could feel a void, a hole.

Early in September, three weeks before my birthday, the pups were born—two females. We wouldn't be able to get the pup until she was six weeks old.

By that time, my life was beginning to fall apart. Shortly after Shane died, I discovered a lump on my pelvis. At first, I thought that I was having some kind of reaction to Shane's death, but I still had it checked out. After several doctors' appointments, I was admitted to the hospital. I had more tests. I was scheduled for surgery two days before we were to pick up the puppy.

The surgeon removed a fibroid tumor, biopsied it, and discovered it to be malignant. It had metastasized to the ovaries. Both ovaries and the uterus were removed. The diagnosis: ovarian cancer.

I was in the hospital and facing chemotherapy treatments. That's a two-year regimen, the oncologist had told me. A lot of things went through my mind. Why me? Why this? Why now? What's going to happen to me? I cried. Now I understood why Betty Rollins titled her book on battling breast cancer *First You Cry* . Then my thoughts went to the puppy we were supposed to get that weekend.

"If I don't go get her, the woman will think that we don't want her," Red said.

"Get her and bring her home, so I will have her to come home to,"

I moaned as I tried to get comfortable in bed. I still had a tube running through my nose into my stomach. I had an incision from my belly button to as far down as possible. A curved piece of something—plastic or plaster of Paris—covered my midsection.

I had heard and read that animals can make recovery easier for humans. I needed that dog. I needed to get better. I was only thirty-nine. I was not ready for my life to be over. I still had too many things to accomplish. Red didn't need this. He'd already lost one wife to a serious disease.

A day later than planned, Red went to get the puppy. I had asked for the smaller of the two and had picked out a name—Lady Bell Star. "Bell Star" was for the motorcycle helmets we wore for protection, and "Lady" was for the fact that I was getting a female.

He brought her home and bathed her under the spigot in the bathtub to get rid of the fleas. He took Polaroid pictures of her on Zeke's little chair and brought the pictures to me in the hospital. I couldn't wait to get home to her.

She took to me immediately, and the feeling was mutual. We got along great. She was definitely my dog, even though she had had about five days with my husband. I needed a dog, especially facing that uphill battle with chemotherapy that would begin in a few days. It was her time to help my healing process.

A few days before my second treatment, I was scheduled to go to the chemo clinic at the hospital. I ran into the woman I'd shared a room with after my surgery. Her name also was Sandy, and we had the same oncologist. She introduced me to another patient in the clinic.

"This is the woman I was in the hospital with," she told her friend. "She was talking one day about her baby, and I figured she had a small child at home and had been diagnosed with cancer. Then she showed me the pictures. It was a dog!"

Star became quite a hit with my coworkers who came to visit and to encourage me to return to work.

"Oh, my gosh," my good friend and coworker Rosemary Armao said when she first saw Star. "I've thrown out cotton balls bigger than that."

She probably did, too, being the mother of two preschool-aged boys.

We lived on the far west side of Franklin County, and almost everyone I worked with lived far to the east or up north. "You have to come back to work because we're tired of driving out here," was their argument. I heeded their good advice and went back to work six weeks after surgery. I think being around this close family of workers aided in my recovery. I was kept busy with a variety of assignments and didn't have time to think about the consequences. I did some small jobs and started writing. The work became therapy, and one lengthy article told of my ordeal.

When I completed the lengthy story, the bureau manager, John Kady, said, "I knew you would write something like that," as he typed my story into that day's budget that tells editors what stories will be transmitted.

John worked out a schedule for me around my chemo treatments so that I wouldn't miss work. I would work Sunday morning, go into the hospital that afternoon, have my treatment on Monday, and come home Tuesday. I could go to work Wednesday if I felt like it. If I did work Wednesday, I could do anything I wanted to. I had regular assignments on Fridays and Saturdays. I had treatments every three or four weeks.

Meanwhile, Star was growing and becoming acquainted with her companion, Zeke. They hit it off well. He would watch over her from a perch just out of reach. When she figured out how to get up on the couch, he moved to the armrest. When she figured out how to get on the armrest, he moved to the top of the couch.

It wasn't long until I knew that Star would make a good mother. After all, the main reason we got the female was to raise a litter of pups.

Star would lie on my lap and lick my legs (when I wore shorts). If she couldn't lick my legs, she licked her own little legs until the white, curly fur turned a rust color.

The first time she came into heat, we decided not to breed her. She was too young. I had bought little doggie diapers to put on her at that time. She didn't like them. I'd put one on her, and she would lie on a pillow in the corner of the couch and give me the dirtiest look. She would start wiggling, and the next thing I knew, she would jump off the couch and want to play. She had also wiggled out of that diaper. Soon she could get out of them almost as quickly as I put them on her.

When Star came into heat the second time, she was twenty-one months old. It was then that we bred her to Zeke.

Throughout her pregnancy, she was a joy to watch. Every morning, when she came back indoors, she got a vitamin. She loved those vitamins and would beg to get one every time she came inside, but I only gave her one a day.

I don't think she realized the changes in her body and life the way a human mother does at this time. She was built short to the ground. Although toy poodles are ten inches high at the shoulder, she didn't measure up to that because of her short legs. She also carried her puppies low. The day before she delivered (or "whelped," in dog terminology), she ran her good friend and neighbor, Spike, a Doberman pinscher, up and down the fence on the north side of the backyard. Her little swaying belly was a blade of grass from the ground.

During her six-week gestation period, my husband would boast, "Star is going to have two pups, and they are both going to be males."

Wednesday, August 1, 1984—my girlfriend Jean's forty-first birthday—Star went into labor. A big water bubble came out but didn't break. I had never been through anything like that before. What do I do? Help! I had started to get dressed to go to work in the middle of the afternoon when it began. I called Red. He came home to relieve me. I hoped he knew more about it that I did. After all, he had two grown daughters; I'd never had children.

Red had expected to see a puppy by the time he got home, but nothing. We whisked Star off to our vet's office. We had changed vets after we lost Shane. This one was a couple of miles away. He gave her a shot to help speed up delivery, and he told us to bring her back if it didn't work in an hour.

I was about ready to leave for work, and there was still no puppy. Red and Star headed back to the vet's office, and I followed. He pulled his car into the vet's driveway, and that first puppy, a female, was born. Red struggled to get the little one out of the sack and get her breathing, all while trying to get the car parked.

The vet said that everything was fine. Red took the new family home. I went to work. Not long after I arrived at work, Red called. Star had had another female about an hour after the first pup was born. He said that Star still didn't know what to do, and he had to get this one out of the sack. An hour later, I had another call. Another female pup. This time, he said that Star had gotten it out of the sack by herself. She was well on her way to really being a mother to her three pups.

Three females! Red's prediction of two males didn't hold. How much do I trust him as a poodle expert, you ask?

When I arrived home that night after work, I just stared at the dog bed of Mama and the pups. I hoped Star could take care of them properly.

You never know what a light sleeper you are until you have a newborn beside your bed. We put the dog bed beside our bed and tried to sleep. Star made sure that the puppies were fed, bathed, and cuddled.

Mealtime—*slurp, slurp, slurp*. Those puppies were noisy while they ate! Then it was time to bathe them. Again, there was a *slurp, slurp, slurp* noise as Star licked those puppies clean. By this time, the puppies were taking a nap and would work their way to the edge of the big square bed. Star didn't know what to do. She'd reach out and get her children and bring them closer to her. They discovered the food line again. *Slurp, slurp, slurp.*

This routine was repeated all night long.

"Star, let those little ones sleep," I begged. "Get some sleep."

We weren't getting much sleep, either, between the noise from the dog bed and our curiosity as to how she was caring for them.

The next night wasn't much better. In addition to the routine established the first night, Star added a new one. She was gaining confidence. After feeding and bathing the puppies, she figured that they were in fine shape. Suddenly, she was on my husband's side of the bed begging to be put in bed with us.

"Star, where are your babies?" Red asked as he took her around the bed to put her back in hers.

I was already on the floor reaching under the bed to retrieve three sleeping puppies.

She kept this up all night, and it was another night that we didn't get much sleep.

The third night, we had to do something. Everyone needed sleep. We put Star and the puppies in the living room and closed the bedroom door. It wasn't long until we heard a whining and scratching at the door. Opening the door, we found Star and her babies.

After several trips to the living room, Red finally hit upon an idea. He put the puppies and the bed on my side of the bed. I took Star into the living room where we slept on the couch. Sleep at last for everyone.

Saturday morning, we had an appointment with the vet to get the puppies' tails and dewclaws cut. These poodles at birth were a little bigger than white mice, complete with long tails. We put the little ones in a shoe box, and Star climbed in the car by herself as she always did. Off to the vet we went, but not before we put our radio/tape player/ recorder on the windowsill and turned it on to see what kind of reaction we would get from Zeke for being left home alone.

"I hated to wake you two up," Red said as we pulled out of the driveway. "It was the first sleep you two had since Wednesday."

The vet took the shoe box of puppies into another room while we held Star on the examining table, petted her, and assured her that her puppies were fine. A few minutes later, the vet came back with the little ones, the pieces of cotton at the tips of their little tails spotted with a little blood. He checked Star.

"Everyone looks good," he said.

Zeke was so happy to see us when we came home. He looked the shoe box over carefully to make sure that we'd brought all of his children home. We rewound the tape and played it back. What horrible moaning and crying we heard. Then a *spizt* sound.

"What was that?" an astonished Red asked as he played that section back a couple of times.

"Oh," I said. "That was Zeke's way of letting us know that he didn't like being left home alone."

He had lifted his leg on the radio/tape player/recorder.

The M and Ms

Here we are, watching three toy poodle puppies grow. We were really expecting two—at least that's what my husband had predicted. We were ready to raise two, but with three … what do we do now? Red settled that problem right away. He named the third one and had a name in mind for the second before I came home from work that evening. He had fallen for the first one because of all of the troubles with her birth.

He quickly became attached to all three. With names for two of them, I had to help come up with a name for that first one. He was watching pups two and three quite a bit, so I figured the firstborn was going to be mine.

These pups were so cute. They started life looking like big white mice. Having their tails and dewclaws cut when they were three days old didn't bother them. Even though their eyes weren't open, they could explore within the confines of their light-blue plastic bed with an old towel for comfort.

The third born appeared to be Red's favorite. The birth was so easy, and Star knew what to do by then. The puppy had a name right away: Misty. Red said that he named her from the movie *Play Misty for Me*. I preferred the song to the movie.

The firstborn dog, the biggest at birth, didn't grow much, but the second born did. The second pup also had a name by the time I arrived home from work that night. Maggie was named for the place we enjoyed so much a month or so before on vacation—Maggie Valley, North Carolina—the first place we saw after driving through the Great Smoky Mountains. We parked our motor home in a campground where we could see the railroad cars going up the hill—or mountain—to an amusement park. We had spent several days in that area.

Naming dogs is an art with Red, I found out. Jacques Pierre, the patriarch of the clan, had a typical name for a French poodle, even though the breed is German by ancestry. Shane got his name from the Alan Ladd movie, one of Red's favorites. I named Star.

Zeke, the father of these pups, got his name because it sounded right, and he really needed a name. I couldn't keep on calling him Big Foot.

The firstborn pup went through a few days without a name. We toyed with Carla, because she was born in the car, but it didn't go with Maggie and Misty. Finally, we settled on Molly, because it sounded appropriate. Molly, Maggie, and Misty.

I remember that my mother wanted to name my brother with the same initials that I have, but my dad nixed that.

"What would you do about mail addressed to the house with just initials?" he asked. "Would you know who to give it to?"

He had a point. At work, I typed high school basketball boxes where siblings were playing. How confusing it was just to use last names. I had to use first initials—and sometimes the first two letters of the first name.

Now what did I do? I'd allowed the dogs to be named with the same letter. They became the three Ms, or the M and Ms—Molly Bee, Maggie Belle, and Misty Star.

All of that attention went to the triplets, as we called them. Maybe Zeke was not getting all that he thought he deserved.

The pups were only a few days old when Red heated a couple of slices of roast beef on a paper plate in the microwave for a sandwich. He put the paper plate on the floor for Zeke to lick up the residue from the roast beef. What a treat!

By the time Red finished his sandwich and reached down for the plate, half of it was gone. Zeke had eaten it. That paper plate didn't digest well. It meant a quick trip to the vet.

He was given a special laxative. It came in a tube. It was dark brown like molasses, thick like molasses, and it smelled like it too. We squeezed some onto a finger and let Zeke lick it. He loved it. We'd give him a little about every hour and then take him for a walk.

We faced a slight problem. We were getting ready to go to Plain City, thirty miles away, for weekend motorcycle races. The day we were getting ready to leave, the pups opened their eyes. We were still giving Zeke his special medication.

"Put 'em all in the motor home, and we'll do the best we can," I said.

Zeke and Star loved to go in the motor home. They had their own places. Zeke jumped up on the couch. Star would sit beside me in my seat. They were good traveling dogs. Even Jacques and Shane before them were great when it came to traveling, even though Jacques didn't live long enough to see a motor home.

The dog bed of puppies fit under the table in the motor home. The pups climbed over the edges of the bed and scouted out their new environment.

In between giving Zeke his laxative and watching him closely in the backyard, I loaded the motor home before I went to work. Red and the dogs would go to Plain City when he came home. By this time, Red had moved into a middle-management position in security with the bank, was working normal hours Monday through Friday, and wearing real clothes rather than uniforms. My hours at UPI still didn't mesh with his. It was strange how both of us worked for companies that required round-the-clock work.

I drove over to Plain City when I left work around 11:00 p.m. It was my turn to work with Zeke. About halfway through the weekend, the laxative finally worked, and he passed that paper plate.

Lesson learned! Never give him anything to eat on a paper plate. That paper was harder on him than the rubber toys he ate.

When he was little, he chewed on his rubber toys and swallowed pieces of rubber. The soft rubber resembled a balloon, and he would leave colorful deposits in the backyard. The hard rubber could have caused a problem going through his system. He once bit off a chunk of a hard rubber toy, but he coughed it up. When I realized that he was eating that type of rubber and bites of that size, I decided that enough was enough.

"Zeke, find something else to play with," I said.

We'd taken away the stuffed elephant, and now we took away the rubber toys. We hadn't had any problems with the other dogs and rubber toys. I hadn't had to worry about the toys with squeakers. When Shane played with those toys, instead of gnawing and getting the squeaker out and possibly swallowing it, he had figured out how to get the squeaker inside the toy.

Star had a pair of socks Red had given her when he brought her home. He rolled these red socks into a ball. She figured out how to get them unrolled, and she made a game of unrolling them as fast as we could roll them. We tied the socks together, and she learned how to get the knot out. She had created a new game. Then she added tug-of-war. That only tightened the knot.

We'd call her toy "red tockies," and she knew what that meant. She'd run to get the red socks and bring them to us so that we could play with her. They began to get ratty and dirty, but she loved them.

I worried the day the socks accidentally were washed. I didn't know it until they fell out of the dryer as I was folding clothes. The red sock was like a child's security blanket—or "banky," as Red's daughter Marsha had called hers. Would Star accept that clean-smelling sock? Would she be mad because I'd washed it? I didn't mean to, but she didn't notice. She still played with it. She hadn't missed it.

The triplets didn't really pick out anything special to play with. They had one another.

We now had five dogs. I could never have parted with any of them.

If anyone had told me that my life would be ruled by dogs, I would have laughed. But here I was, doing everything for them. It seemed that they came first. My life had gone to the dogs.

Maggie

The three girls developed distinct personalities and traits as they grew. Maggie, the second born, became the largest of the three and used that size to her advantage. She became the litter boss and let everyone know it. She did a lot of barking—*loud* barking. She was the loudest dog we ever had.

When the pups were five months old, Red had another bout with what we thought was stomach flu. It had crept up at busy periods and put a crimp in our plans. Each time, it seemed worse. This time, the illness hit him right after Christmas and sent him to the hospital, where he was diagnosed with hepatitis B. Tracing the history of his flare-ups, the doctors and I figured that he had been carrying it for a long time. Perhaps he had come into contact with some bad blood when he handled traffic crashes in the patrol. The officers didn't wear rubber or latex gloves in those days.

The illness seemed to hit around a stressful time. He had just gone through a budget-writing process at work. After a week in the hospital, he used the recliner in the living room as a place of recovery, trying to regain his strength. It was a cold January. Temperatures were in the double digits below zero.

While Red recuperated, the triplets spent their time in the kitchen behind a baby gate. He tried his best to care for the dogs while I was at work. Those little ones were a challenge—feeding them, putting them outside, giving them the attention that he thought they deserved—and then there was their annoying barking.

When he put all of the dogs out at the same time, they'd do their business and come up the back steps quickly. They didn't like being outside any more than necessary—all except Maggie. She would run into the middle of the backyard and stand there waiting for Red to come and get her—and she did it regardless of the weather.

"That dog doesn't have enough sense to come in out of the rain," I always said.

The barking bothered Red. "Maggie, pipe down!" he'd shout. Nothing seemed to work. "Maggie, if you don't shut up, I'm going to box you up and send you to Cincinnati," he threatened.

Red had friends near Cincinnati. In his second marriage, he and his wife Joyce had two dogs, Ginger and Jacques. When Joyce died, he decided that having two dogs was too much. He gave Ginger to friends who later moved to Cincinnati. They took excellent care of Ginger, and she lived a long life.

Maggie must have understood. Not only did she quiet down, but she also crawled on Red's lap and clung to him—not just once, but for nearly fourteen more years.

"Are you sure she isn't attached to you with Velcro?" I often asked.

When any other dog tried to get close to Red, Maggie would come running and wiggle between them.

"I've never seen a dog so possessive of a human," Red said.

As the girls grew, Molly began looking like the character Gizmo from the movie *Gremlins*. I started to call her Gizmo, but Red wouldn't let me continue.

"She'll grow up and not know what her name is," he said.

So Molly it was. And Maggie. But Misty often got called Mittie.

Maggie developed a funny trait. Female dogs will squat—or drop their back legs and nearly sit on the ground—to relieve themselves. Not Maggie. She acted as if she didn't want to contaminate her bottom. Instead, she anchored her front feet on the ground and lifted her hind end and folded her back legs close to her body. She once got so high that I thought she would stand on her nose. I never did take a picture of her. To me, that would have been an invasion of her privacy. A few people laughed at her.

When the girls were a little over a year old, Maggie got away from me at the wrong time. We had decided not to spay them, and now we were going to pay the price. Zeke was that stud dog his father Jacques was, and now we were about to have another litter of pups.

Red yelled at me. He told me that I had to find homes for these pups, because we couldn't handle any more dogs. We already had five dogs.

Maggie wasn't anything like Star. Maggie didn't want her daily vitamin. She carried her pups high. It was hard to tell that she was pregnant.

Her litter was born early in the morning of January 21, 1986. Red helped deliver the first one, but I had to be midwife the rest of the morning, because he had to go to work.

Zeke lay on the bed and watched. The other dogs stayed out of the bedroom. I sat on the floor beside the dog bed. Maggie would lie on my lap until she was ready to deliver a pup, and then she'd crawl into that light-blue plastic dog bed. She seemed to know when they were coming.

She had three males and one female that morning. What do I do with four pups? The last born was a big one—much bigger than any I had seen—and I had now seen seven pups at birth or shortly thereafter.

When Red came home and saw our new litter, he changed his mind. He fell for that big male and immediately named him Jacques Andre after our first two dogs. You don't name a dog you're going to find a new home for. I had to find a home for three.

Big Jacques seemed to take over the food line. The second born, the first one I oversaw the delivery of, couldn't get to the food line and was getting cold. We wrapped him in a washcloth and placed him on a heating pad. We'd put him close to Maggie in the hopes that he would eat.

"Don't get attached to him," the vet advised us during that first visit—the one where the tails and dewclaws are cut.

But how can you not get attached to a little one that you are keeping warm and fed? All of that work we did helped. He ate and grew stronger. He also got a name—Pete, short for Peter John.

That was a name I always liked after having seen the movie and read the book *A Man Called Peter,* which is the story of Presbyterian minister Peter Marshall. The son's name was Peter John, and I liked the actor who portrayed him and the role he'd played. I'd vowed that if I ever had the opportunity to name a son, I would choose Peter John. Having children was out of the question, so the best I could do was name a dog.

We worried about how the other dogs would react, especially Star, who had already had one litter. The vet had talked with us about false pregnancies, since the triplets had come into heat at the same time. We didn't really need to worry. Star didn't pay attention to the new additions, and neither did Molly.

We kept Maggie and the pups in the dog bed at the end of the hallway in front of the full-length mirror. Occasionally, we would find the dog bed partway to the living room.

I didn't move it. Red said that he didn't move it. We respected Maggie and the job she was doing feeding her family. The bed was about five feet from the wall. I'd put it back. It happened several times. We finally did catch the culprit—and caught her in action. Misty!

She was the one going through a false pregnancy. Her desire to have pups was strong. She grabbed hold of one corner of the bed and dragged it down the hall.

We had a wire cage that we used when traveling. We brought that cage upstairs, put a little soft throw rug in the bottom, and put Misty and the little unnamed female in there. Misty was happy. She took care of that little puppy. She even had a little bit of milk, but not enough to sustain the puppy. We didn't name the third male or the female, because I had a lead on someone who wanted one of them.

By the time the little ones were six weeks old and went back to the vet for their checkups and shots, they were all doing well.

"This is the one you said not to get attached to," I told the vet, holding up a squiggly Pete, now well filled out and showing no evidence of not being able to find the food line a few weeks earlier.

The four little ones got a clean bill of health. I called the woman who was interested in a pup. She came out and looked at them. We had held Jacques Andre and Pete back, leaving her to choose from the male and the female. She chose the male. Not long afterward, she called and asked if she could have the female too. She returned the next day and took the female.

I did it! I found a home for two pups. It was a nice home. We kept in touch with the adopters and visited occasionally. Jacques, Pete, and Maggie never showed any indication that those two pups were part of their family.

We didn't sell the dogs; Red said that you don't sell children. It wasn't a giveaway, but more of an adoption—and an open adoption at that. The people were aware of the parentage.

We now had seven dogs between the ages of six weeks and twelve years! Were we crazy?

Maggie's Pups

Maggie's job of mothering was almost over. The two remaining pups were exploring and eating regular food. Maggie returned to Red's lap.

It was fun to again watch pups grow. We could almost see Jacques Andre grow. He was big to start with. He had long legs. It seemed his legs grew, and then as he began to grow, his legs continued to grew. That was like his father, Zeke, only it was Zeke's feet that seemed bigger than normal.

Although toy poodles are ten inches high at the shoulders, Jacques' legs alone were longer.

"He's got his grandmother's legs," I said.

"Can't be," Red said. "Star had short legs."

"That's right. Jacques has *her* legs."

He wasn't the most graceful dog. He had to learn to adjust to his size.

"What's that big thing prancing around your backyard like he owns it?" my neighbor Ron Ratliff asked one day when we ran into each other at the corner convenience store.

"That's Maggie's baby," I said. "And yes, he does think that he owns the place."

Because of Jacques' size, he must have thought that he was "cock of the walk." Even though he was much bigger than the other dogs, he was gentle. All of the dogs got alone fine. At their full size, the other dogs could walk underneath Jacques, and it didn't bother him.

One time, I caught him sitting on a step with all four feet on the step below. He looked so funny.

Every once in a while, Maggie snarled at him.

"Mother is putting him in his place," Red would say. "She knows she's his mother, and she's the boss."

She never did anything like that to Pete. And Star didn't tangle with her girls. I guess Maggie had to take Jacques down to size occasionally. Maggie never cut the skin when she snarled at him.

A couple of times, when the triplets were young, Maggie and Misty jumped Molly and left her with a cut, which I quickly cleaned with hydrogen peroxide. One of the cuts was on her rump. Hair grew in around that cut in a champagne color and in the shape of a saddle. It didn't take long for that beige spot to turn white again.

Only once in all of the years that Red had dogs did any of them bite him, and that was before I met him. Red was down at Jacques Pierre's level and playing with him like he was going to eat his food. Jacques lunged at him and nipped him on the nose. It drew blood, and Red had to get a couple of stitches and a tetanus shot. Jacques was under quarantine.

From the left: Misty, Zeke, Star, Pete,
Molly, Maggie, and Jacques Andre

Dogs Are Almost Human

I've seen a lot of studies that place poodles high on the intelligence list. Usually, border collies are tops, and poodles are not far behind. Our dogs never ceased to amaze me with their intelligence.

"At times, they scare me," I often said.

Sports played a big role in our lives. Since we met on the night of a baseball all-star game, I always used that as our anniversary. Red, I think, remembers the date better than I do. I have to check a calendar on the computer for the exact date.

I love baseball, and in the seventh grade, I wanted to be a baseball announcer. My father had said that if I wanted to be a baseball announcer, I had to learn journalism. I started looking into that field and got a job that fall as an area correspondent to the *Bucyrus Telegraph-Forum*, our local newspaper. That was the start of my writing career.

Basketball was one of my family's nights out for entertainment. I can remember going to basketball games at the local school even before I started school. When I was in high school, baseball and basketball were the only sports our little school offered.

Red had played basketball in high school in the early 1940s. It was the only sport offered at his little school.

"Did you play full court or half court?" I teased.

"It wasn't that long ago," he snipped.

As soon as we discovered that we had a mutual love of the game, he asked his oldest brother, Horace, a graduate of The Ohio State University, to apply for basketball season tickets and give him the form. That was our entry to OSU basketball for thirty years. Over the years, our seat assignments kept getting higher and higher in the stands until I could almost reach the rafters if I stretched high enough. I suppose that if we had made sizeable contributions to the university, we would have had better seats.

I worked on nights of many OSU roads games, and Red watched the games on television. If I wasn't working, we could watch the road games together.

One night, when I was working at UPI and Red was watching a road game, an Ohio State player missed two foul shots—not unusual, but frustrating.

"Missed 'em both," he said disgustedly, putting emphasis on "*missed.*"

The word "Mistress" was a magical word in the household. When we talked to the dogs, we always referred to each other as Master or Mistress. At the sound of *missed*, Jacques Pierre, Shane, and Zeke woke up and ran to the front door, apparently thinking that he was going to say, "Mistress home," the signal for them to form a welcoming committee at the front door.

This was before reporters and stringers had portable computers and could file stories from the scene. The person working the main desk had to take dictation from reporters or stringers covering events.

A stringer is similar to a freelance reporter. He or she isn't employed by the newspaper or wire service but will work for them on certain occasions. The person could be employed by a newspaper that subscribed to the UPI service and provided stories for the wire service. The person would also receive a small fee for the work.

In those days, stringers phoned their notes or stories in to the person on the desk. The Radio Shack TRS-80 wasn't in use then. (That was a word processor where reporters could write the story, hook up to a telephone, and send the story to the office.) The person who worked the main desk would take the dictation from the reporter. Taking these calls for a good ten years, I could type about as fast as the reporter could dictate.

One night, I was taking dictation from Dick Svoda, a sports writer from the now-defunct *Cleveland Press* who was stringing the Cleveland Cavaliers. In describing a turning point in the game, he used the phrase "missed them both," and I broke out laughing. I apologized and explained why I laughed. He, too, joined in the laughter.

I also liked music, thanks in part to taking piano lessons all through my school years. I never grew into an accomplished pianist, but it was enough to teach me a love of music. I played E-flat alto horn and later

French horn in our school band. My love of music genres stretches from classical through old standards, through early days of rock and roll, and through legendary country.

I like to sing, and I know that I'm not the world's best singer. I would sing along with the radio when I was alone or when the dogs and I were alone. I knew that they wouldn't boo me off stage. I'd sing some old standards and change the words, inserting their names whenever appropriate. For instance, to the tune of "I Love My Baby (My Baby Loves Me)," I'd make it "I love my doggie, my doggie loves me," or I'd try to stretch "Star" into two syllables.

Another favorite was the Al Jolson standard *Swanee*. I'd sing it "Maggie, how I love you, how I love you, my dear old Maggie." Or Misty or Molly, or Pete-y or Jacques-y. I didn't know how much the dogs understood until one day, a radio station featuring old music played that Al Jolson song. Maggie sat up, perked her ears, and turned toward the speakers. She recognized that song. I just stood there in the living room watching her in awe until the song was over.

Those dogs could provide a lot of laughter—things that make memories. They could also be frustrating at times, but I couldn't get mad at them. They gave us unconditional love. Either one of us could be having a miserable day, but they didn't really know it. They could cheer us up by nothing more than running across the room to get a toy and shaking it, or crawling up on our laps and giving us a kiss.

Author Sandi Latimer and Zeke in summer of 1983
Photo by Sue Ogrocki, used by permission of Sue Ogrocki

Camping

As soon as we bought the motor home, we joined a segment of the population I had often written stories about—campers and the number-one family activity in Ohio. State parks are such popular spots for camping that reservations are not accepted for most sites. It's on a first-come, first-served basis. It wasn't unusual to find the Full sign out by Friday morning. Some people would go to campgrounds on Thursday or come earlier and leave their units. That didn't really seem fair to others. We would get a site and stay there, using that as our home base for as long as we were allowed to stay, and go to work from the campground. We were hooked up to water, sewer, and electric. Since we worked different shifts, the dogs were not left alone for long in the motor home.

Not all campsites offered water, sewer, and electric. Many sites were primitive, meaning that no hookups were available. Even if we didn't have such amenities, we could get along well. We were self-contained. We had a generator that we could use for electricity. We had a full tank of water, and we could use our toilet and drain water into a holding tank. But we'd have to visit the dump site when the tanks were full.

Besides water, sewer, and electric, some campgrounds had other amenities. At the campground in Maggie Valley, North Carolina, in the summer of 1984, we had a cable television hookup. We watched a movie we had already seen but saw a few scenes that weren't considered "family" viewing.

On a trip with friends to Myrtle Beach, South Carolina, we were advised to take along a phone. This was long before everyone carried cell phones. Setting up at our site, we found a phone hookup. We plugged in our phone and ran the cord through the window on the driver's side of the motor home. Our number was the four-digit number of our site.

Since camping was so popular, to make sure that we had a spot in a campground, we bought a membership in Coast to Coast, a company that operates private campgrounds. The closest campground was south of Delaware across the road from Alum Creek State Park and about thirty miles from home. We spent nearly the whole first summer at that campground, moving every week to a different site. Several families were staying there at that time, and it was like playing "upset the apple cart" the day we moved to different sites. We wanted prospective campground membership buyers to see how the members were using the facilities. Red and I learned to play tennis that summer.

In the late summer and early fall of 1984, when the triplets were little, we had the most popular site at the campground. Anytime we had the pups outside, people stopped by and made a fuss over those little ones. We could have given them away several times over, but that was not the intention. We had committed to raising the litter. Besides, we didn't know the people and didn't know what kind of homes they would have provided for the dogs.

In warm months, we spent most of our time at the membership campground. Other campgrounds were added to the program, so we were able to stay at as many as three or four a summer. These campgrounds were not too far from home, which meant that we could go to work from there.

When we were planning a vacation, we purchased blue cards for a dollar a card that allowed us one night per card at another Coast to Coast campground.

The dogs grew to like the motor home and camping almost as much as we did. When I'd start loading the motor home in preparation for a weekend or a week or longer, they'd get excited, knowing that they were going to go with us. They could hardly wait for the jingle of their collars that held their licenses and shot records. They didn't wear the collars around the house; they were put on only when they went beyond our fenced-in backyard at home.

When I took their collars from the nail in the bathroom closet, they'd run to that closet and then to the top step that led from the living room to the front door and wait for me to put their collars on them. Shane would often run around in circles. Their waiting wasn't patient. They'd squirm so much that I could hardly get the collars fastened. As soon as I accomplished that, down the steps they'd bound to the front door, impatiently waiting for me to open the door so that they could run to the motor home parked at the curb in front of the house.

Star usually sat beside me in the passenger's wide, chair-type seat. Most of the others curled up on the floor or jumped up on the couch. Later, they knew what cage they would be in. They'd be asleep in a short time. They were good traveling dogs.

When we were in campgrounds, Red and I took the dogs with us on our walks to get familiar with our surroundings. Their usual spot when we were at the site was on a leash attached to a tie-down stake in front of the motor home. They had enough leeway so that they could be out in the sun and warmth or could get under the awning and into the shade. They could see everything going on, and they loved the attention that they received from passersby.

Most people who'd see them out front or walking with us couldn't tell the dogs apart.

"How do you do it? How can you tell them apart?" were questions we got asked quite a bit.

To myself, I would say, *If you can't tell a male from a female, you're in trouble.* I told those people that each dog has its own personality and even a different texture in hair. And of course, they were all different sizes.

At first, much of the vacation planning was left up to me. Red would make sure that the motor home was in tip-top condition, and I was in charge of the food. When we decided where to go, it was my job as navigator to plan the trip.

I'm glad that he trusted me after my goof at trying to navigate my way from Sandusky to Columbus in the airplane. I knew that I could tune an instrument on the panel to the frequency of a radio station and that would take me to that city. As we left Sandusky one day, I tuned in to a radio station at a city we'd fly over on the way home—only I wasn't flying south as I should have been. I was going east and getting closer to Cleveland. I didn't realize a station in Cleveland enjoyed the same frequency and was much stronger than the one farther south. I'm directionally challenged, both in the air and on the ground! Red corrected me, but he hasn't let me live it down.

When it came time for the 1985 vacation, Red told me to leave the travel planning to him. That meant that I could read a book, knit, or crochet instead of staring at a map and following exit signs as we traveled the freeway.

We headed south. It could have been anywhere, but when we crossed into Florida, I knew that we were headed to Disney World. When we bought the motor home, it had a bumper sticker from a campground near Disney World. Red wanted to go there.

We found the campground and pulled in. I went into the office to inquire about a space for a twenty-seven-foot motor home in the pet area. I was told that the dogs would have to be put in a kennel.

"I'll go in a kennel before they do," I said as I turned around and walked out. "To the next campground," I told Red when I got to my seat. I think the dogs understood what I was going through, because I soon had Star and Molly on my lap, and I gave them a big hug.

The sky was beginning to look like rain, and Red decided to pull into the first campground we came to that accepted pets. We would pay by the day in case we didn't like the campground or we wanted to move on. While I checked a campground on one side of the road, he checked the one on the other side. The one I checked was full. We took the one he checked. I'm glad, because I thought the skies would open any minute. Being from Ohio, I'm accustomed to pop-up afternoon showers, and I felt that we could get one soon.

We found a campsite that was nearly level and had full hookups—water, sewer, and electric. However, we found a limit on the number of pets.

"We'll take them out one at time," Red said. "No one will know that we have five dogs."

The third day we were there, the security guard at the gatehouse at the entrance stopped us as we were driving our tow car to Disney World, and he started chatting with Red. Red pulled the car to the side of the driveway and went back to speak with the guard. I thought the guard was referring to the license plate when he asked if we were from Columbus. The license plate has a sticker designating the county where the car is registered.

A few minutes later, Red returned with a look of astonishment on his face.

"You won't believe it," he started out. "That's Bill."

"Bill who?" I asked. Bill is quite a common name.

The guard was my husband's first wife's current boyfriend, and we had all sat in the same pew several months earlier at the wedding of my husband's younger daughter, Marlene.

"Oh, my gosh!" I said, drawing out every word.

"Alice's sister Marilyn is the park manager," he said. "I haven't seen her in twenty-five years."

"What are the odds of that happening?" I asked.

Alice was Red's first wife.

I dismissed the oddity and enjoyed the day at Disney World. When we returned in midafternoon, I stayed at the motor home to take care of the dogs and start dinner while Red went up to the office to pay another day's fees and to share some time with his ex-sister-in-law. I didn't care how long he was gone. After all, two people who haven't seen each other in twenty-five years can have a lot to talk about.

I didn't feel intimidated or threatened by the presence of his ex-family. He'd been away from them for many years. The girls were adults now. Everyone had accepted me as the newest member of the family.

Saturday morning, we went to the activity building for a campground-wide breakfast, and Alice was cooking breakfast.

I knew we weren't going to have any problem with how many dogs we had even though the conversation started with Alice asking how the dogs were.

"They're having fun and think of the motor home as their second home," I told her.

We put quite a few miles on that motor home—trips to Cape Cod, Massachusetts; Mountain View, Arkansas; Branson, Missouri—but with all of the dogs and spending so much time from May to October in that small space, we decided that it was time to trade up.

We looked at a thirty-seven-foot Allegro, the same one we had seen the previous winter at the local boat and RV show. We decided to buy it. We came back from the dealer's showroom/lot that Saturday morning in the spring of 1987 and started to clean out the Sprinter.

We hauled out the specially made mattress and reinstalled the original cushions and table in the back. All of the dishes, cookware, clothing, tools, tennis rackets, and ball gloves came out and were piled in the basement, the living room, or wherever we could put them.

All the while, Zeke lay on the top step of the living room watching us.

"Zeke, we're not getting rid of your second home," I told him, rubbing his topknot. I made another trip to get more items from the motor home. "We're getting you a new home."

I passed Red on that trip. "Zeke's crying," I said. "Real tears too."

"I'll have a talk with him," Red said.

Zeke seemed to know a lot. So did the others, but how much, I could only guess.

We drove the Sprinter to the dealer's lot, handed over the keys, took the new ones, and headed home. Red hooked up the car behind the new motor home, gave me the keys, and said, "Let's go for a drive."

I took off slowly. It was like driving a semitruck. I took some back roads to get a feel for handling it. It wasn't really that hard to drive. I knew that I wasn't going to be passing anyone, and I wasn't going to be parking it. That was up to Red.

The first summer that we had the Allegro, we went back to the Ozarks in central Missouri and on to Tulsa, Oklahoma. Zeke was getting up in years. He was thirteen, sixty-eight years in human life. His circulatory system was failing him. He'd be all right, and then suddenly he'd fall flat on his belly. I'd pick him up, hold him, and rub his belly. He'd perk up again. I always feared that one time, he wouldn't come back. I didn't think that I could handle that.

He fell down on me once on that trip, but he perked up, and I told him to hold on until we got home. I began to realize that he wouldn't be with us much longer. I had always worried what we would do if we lost a dog while traveling. If that happened, I would have cleaned out the ice maker, put the dog's body in a plastic bag, and stuffed it in the ice maker until we got home and could bury it in its proper place. I never did ask Red what he would do. It was something that I didn't feel comfortable talking about.

We returned home late on a Sunday afternoon. I had a mammogram first thing Monday morning at the hospital about a mile from us. When I got back from the hospital, Red met me at the front door.

"Zeke's gone," he said soberly.

I had forgotten to tell Zeke to hold on for me when I left for the hospital.

Allegro Club

Not long after getting the new motor home, Roy Jones from the Central Ohio Allegro Club called us and encouraged us to join their group. All of the members had Allegro motor homes. We'd get a call every month from Roy telling us where the group would be camping that weekend. After a couple of these calls, we decided that we would go meet these people. We soon joined the club and went to the campouts one weekend a month.

Besides going to a campground once a month with the Central Ohio Allegro Club for socialization, we had the opportunity to go to a rally that the manufacturer organized every year. The first one we attended was in Gulf Shores, Alabama, along the Gulf of Mexico. The motor home was made in Red Bay, Alabama, in the northwest corner of the state. It wasn't too far from the factory and not too far for the people at the national level to organize activities for us.

Our club caravanned to Alabama for the weeklong rally. As our motor homes rolled down the road that paralleled the Gulf of Mexico, I became excited at my surroundings.

"Look at the sand," I said excitedly, pointing to white hills along the road. "It looks like snowdrifts with grass growing out of them."

Red didn't share my enthusiasm. "I'm trying to drive and keep my eyes on the road," he said sternly. "Your job is to navigate for me. They'll be plenty of time for sightseeing. Just help me get to the state park."

Even though we were in a caravan, we were not traveling closely together. Each of us had a set of directions. I helped guide Red to the state park and a site. He backed the motor home into the site and leveled the vehicle. Without being level, the propane wouldn't flow from the tank to the kitchen appliances.

The leaders of the national organization planned workshops at which they showed new equipment and how to use it. Cooking demonstrations showed us how to use the new oven that was a combination microwave/convection. We also had time to mingle with people from all over the country—and, of course, that number-one activity: sightseeing. Or was it sampling area restaurants?

On that trip, several of the central Ohio members had dinner together one night at a nearby restaurant, and most of us drove a few miles east into Pensacola and visited the museum at the naval air station.

Campsites in this state park were practically level. We didn't have to run up on many boards to level one side or the other or one wheel more than another. One unusual thing that I noticed was the tall pine trees. They didn't provide much shade, since their limbs were so high. Those trees also had huge pine cones. A previous camper had left a couple on the picnic table. They were about as big around as a salad plate. In the middle of the night, a pine cone fell off the tree and landed on the top of our rig with a sound that I thought was a gunshot. I was out of the bed and halfway down the hallway, shaking.

"What was that?" I trembled.

"Just a pine cone," Red said. "Now come back to bed."

The next day, as we prepared to take the dogs for a walk, Red said to leave Pete in the motor home. I didn't understand Red's reasoning, but I went along with him. We walked past John and Dotty Billman's rig. John was outside as we walked by. He counted dogs. "You're one dog short," he said.

"Yep," Red said calmly. "Alligators got Pete last night."

"You're kidding!" was John's shocked reply. By then, Red and I couldn't keep quiet any longer. We broke out laughing.

Another year, we left a club campout in the Hocking Hills of south central Ohio and drove to a rally in a caravan to Renfro Valley in southern Kentucky. I remembered listening to a radio program when I was a child that was broadcast from Renfro Valley. It was a combination of country music and church service. We looked it up one time when my family was on vacation, and Mom was disappointed. We saw a barn that had RENFRO VALLEY painted on the roof. "I thought it would be bigger," she said of the grounds that held that barn where the radio program was produced and the ever-present gift shop.

A few changes had been made over the years. A campground had been added, and the radio program now came from a barn-like building that had a comfortable auditorium setting. The gift shop had expanded to several little shops. Restaurants and a big building where many of the rally workshops were held had been built across the road.

Dogs were always welcome at these events. We wouldn't have gone if they couldn't go. We put them outside as soon as we were parked and settled. They were an attention getter as we walked them throughout the campgrounds. I don't think the dogs had any idea where they were. All they knew was that they were with Master and Mistress and had traveled in the motor home.

Merry Christmas

My first year with dogs—Jacques and Shane, specifically—was what I considered a normal Christmas. Red had purchased the house in November and had moved in Thanksgiving weekend. I slowly moved my things in after the holidays.

I was looking forward to Christmas. Ever since I'd moved out on my own in September 1966, I'd always bought a cut tree and decorated it, even though it was only me, and I was far removed from childhood. I did the same thing for the holidays of 1973—bought the tree, hauled it to the house, and put it in the back stairwell.

A couple of days later, Red took the tree inside, put it in the stand, and added some water. The tree stood in front of the ceiling-to-floor window in the living room, and the television was moved to one side.

I strung lights and hung ornaments, taking care to put nonbreakable ones on the bottom limbs, and then I draped tinsel. I stood back to admire my work. No dog around me.

I gathered the boxes and took them downstairs to the storage space under the steps. Climbing the steps to the living room, I could see without being heard or hardly seen. Shane was sitting under the tree, batting a nonbreakable ornament on a low limb.

I fretted for the couple of weeks that the tree was up. I feared that the dogs would knock it over. I tried to keep Shane away even though the nonbreakable items were within his paw's reach; Jacques was more reserved and didn't get near the tree.

The next year, I put a short tree on a card table in the front window. It didn't look right, and it didn't seem right, either.

"What do you enjoy more—the dogs or the tree?" Red asked.

"That's easy," I said. "The dogs."

By now, we had three dogs—Jacques, Shane, and Zeke.

The following year, we had no tree, but I did put decorations on the window and on the mirror over the sofa. Of course, stockings were hung with care on the railing between the living room and the steps going down to the front door. I put up a stocking for each member of the household, both four-legged and two-legged.

It seemed a little strange without a tree, but we managed. After all, we were well into adulthood and had no two-legged children. Besides, I didn't have to worry about a dog tipping over a tree.

That was the year that I decided to make dog biscuit wreaths. I had seen them in a gift catalogue for around twenty dollars. I figured that I could make them for much less.

Three Styrofoam wreath forms, a roll of red plastic ribbon, and a box of Milk Bone dog biscuits didn't come anywhere near twenty dollars, plus tax and shipping and handling. It took me a while, but I finally learned how to anchor the ribbon, wrap it, and insert dog biscuits as I wrapped.

Christmas morning, I put their wreaths on the floor along with their stockings that contained rubber toys.

Shane and Zeke figured out how to get the dog biscuits out of the wreaths—they just grabbed a biscuit and shook the wreaths. Jacques tried, but he was over ten years of age and had lost a few teeth. In human years, he would have been in his midfifties.

I made a wreath for each dog each year until the triplets came. I continued to make three wreaths. They'd have to learn to share.

Misty developed her own way of freeing a biscuit from the wreath. She'd put her foot on the wreath to anchor it and then pull on a dog bone. She always put a foot on the plate or in the bowl of food so that it wouldn't get away from her.

Somehow, a dog always seemed to get a wreath around his or her neck. They looked cute.

The year after I first made the wreaths, I decided that instead of a dog toy in the stockings, I would put dog food in the plastic breakaway Easter eggs and put those in the stockings.

Each dog had a stocking with eggs, and we'd watch as they'd work the eggs out, roll them, hear the rattling of dog food, and bite the eggs to open them to reveal the contents.

In the early days, Zeke would break open the eggs, and food would scatter. Shane liked the Bonz, Purina's roundish-shaped dog food with a soft center, and would slap them around like they were hockey pucks.

By the time we had Star, her three daughters, and her two grandsons, the Christmas ritual was fun to watch.

I'd put the stockings on the floor. All the dogs would jump on the couch and watch Star. She'd nose the eggs out of the stockings. She'd empty every stocking and round up all of the eggs. She was the dog with the best set of teeth; she could get her mouth around the egg and chomp down hard enough to break it open to expose its contents. As the other dogs found what they wanted, they'd pounce on the dog food.

Misty, who had a sturdy build like a bulldog, acted as though food was precious and as if she couldn't get enough. She was always burying the dry dog food in the afghan, under the seat cushions of the couch, or in the blankets in the dog beds. I'd find a handful of dog food when I cleaned under the cushions. When I'd fold the afghan or dog blankets, dog food would fly everywhere. I would have to get the yardstick and bat the food out from under the couch.

The stockings held around eight eggs, and I'd fix a stocking for every dog—at one time we had seven dogs. That was more than fifty eggs of food. At the end of the day, we'd scoop up leftover food and put it back in the eggs, and then we'd put the eggs down for them the next day. It seemed we had Christmas every day for at least a week. They played with the eggs as much as they played with toys or their food.

By the time I retrieved all of the egg halves, I didn't put them too far out of sight. After all, I had to fill them again. Only this time, they went into Easter baskets.

Making Dog Biscuit Wreaths

Items needed:

Styrofoam wreath form
Roll of wide plastic ribbon or grosgrain ribbon, preferably red
Milk Bone dog biscuits
Stapler or glue gun

Anchor the end of the ribbon to the wreath form with a stapler. Start wrapping the ribbon around the wreath form. At the start of the second wrap, hold a dog biscuit in place and wrap the ribbon over it tightly enough to hold it in place. One half of the biscuit will be showing. At every other wrap, put in a dog biscuit. To finish off after the last wrap, cut the ribbon from the roll and anchor it on the underside of the wreath with a stapler.

A glue gun can be used if you are using grosgrain ribbon.
This is an ideal gift for a small dog.

Birthdays

irthdays provided a lot of fun too. I think Red had about as much fun as the dogs. For one thing, he knew more about what was going on than the dogs did. It was he who insisted on having a little party. He'd never let me forget a birthday. With several dogs, we had birthday parties quite often.

At first, when I mixed up the cake batter, I made it into cupcakes. Since Red couldn't digest chocolate, I always bought a white or a yellow cake mix. It's strange that the best cake I could make from scratch was chocolate, and I'd married a man who couldn't handle chocolate. Dogs aren't supposed to have chocolate either, so they couldn't lick the bowl or mixer beaters, or even have a piece of the cake. Butterscotch cake mixes weren't popular with anyone but me.

For the first few years, I'd put a cupcake on a plate for each dog and let him eat it. One year, I tried putting ribbons on paper cups and tying them under the dogs' chins. They didn't take too well to those birthday hats. They lasted as long as I could take a picture. The cupcakes didn't last much longer either.

I quickly learned to spread newspapers on the floor before I put the cake plates down. It was easier to clean afterward.

The fun quotient increased as the number of dogs increased. Misty was also fun to watch.

"She'd eat anything that didn't eat her first," was Red's description of her. Her foot was in the middle of the plate as she gobbled up the cake.

Maggie was the picky one. She'd sniff food several times before taking a bite—if the other dogs didn't barge in and steal it from her.

"She acts like she doesn't trust me," Red would say.

It didn't take the dogs long to devour the treats. At times, I made a cake and cut them small pieces, and Red and I would get ours too.

Sometimes, we could have the party on the back patio, but for Zeke, who was born in December, and Maggie's pups, which came along in January, that was out of the question.

There were times when Red would go to the neighborhood supermarket and purchase a cake from the bakery. Those bakeries could provide some exquisite delicacies, and I really hated to cut them.

I often wondered if the dogs got a sugar high as kids do, or if the sugar had any effect on the glucose in their blood. I do know that they had messy faces, but that was quickly taken care of. Molly, who acted as though she wanted to be everyone's friend, would go from dog to dog to lick the frosting from their faces.

I think she got that from me, because I clean up the leftover frosting and crumbs after serving the cake. I always said that crumbs didn't contain calories. But the dogs didn't clean the crumbs off the rug.

Grooming

The poodle is a breed of dog that doesn't shed its hair. That was one help in keeping the house and motor home clean. A dog that doesn't shed is the only kind of dog Red would have. He doesn't like dog hair all over the place. The woman he bought the house from had owned a long-haired black dog. What a mess we had to clean when we started moving in. We found so much dog hair in the drain in the basement stairwell outdoors that I'm surprised the drain wasn't clogged and the basement flooded.

Not shedding puts poodles into one category with humans. Just as we go to the hairdresser or barbershop on a regular basis to get our hair cut or trimmed, poodles also regularly go to a groomer to have their hair cut.

If I keep my hair short, I can go a couple of months or so before my hair gets too long and starts to bother me. The dogs also began to look a little shaggy about every two months. That meant a trip to the Latimer Barber and Beauty Shop in our basement.

Many poodle owners, as well as owners of other dogs that don't shed, choose to send their pets to a groomer. Red started out sending his dogs, Ginger and Jacques, to a groomer, but he quickly discovered that some groomers weren't too handy with the trimmers, or the blades were dull, or the dogs misbehaved. The dogs came away with a botched trim job. He didn't like the way the groomer did his dogs. He decided that he would do his own grooming.

He bought a set of clippers and a couple of blades and learned how to cut the dogs' hair the way he wanted them to look. He did a good job, because when he would be out and about with the dogs, people would comment on how good the dogs looked and wanted to know where he had them groomed.

"You will get more business than you can handle," is his advice to people wanting to start a dog-grooming business.

And you will get more headaches too. As he learned from others how to cut the dogs' hair, he also learned that some people didn't care for their dogs the way he did. Some poodles didn't get a daily brushing and combing or a bath on a regular basis. The hair became tangled and matted.

He had a full-time job. Dog grooming could have turned into another full-time job. That's when he began teaching others how to groom dogs.

We always tried to schedule the grooming sessions on days when I either didn't have to work or would work a late shift.

I made a sling for the dogs from remnants of sturdy material I'd bought at a nearby fabric store. I cut holes for the legs, one scallop for the neck, and another one for the tail. I trimmed it with bias tape. I put grommets in the corners and tied long shoelaces so that Red could hang it from C hooks at a height where he could easily work.

He'd start with the oldest and work his way down. When the dog was finished, he or she would race up the steps and hope that I offered sympathy. It seemed as though they wanted to say, "Mistress, help me. Protect me from Master."

I'd make over the trimmed dog and assure him or her that things were okay. Then I'd locate the next in line and take him or her down for the next appointment. It took Red about an hour and a half to do each dog. No wonder it took two days to do all of the dogs.

Normally, he wouldn't groom a pup until it was six months old, but he gave Shane a poodle cut right before I met him. Zeke didn't get his first trim until he was six months old, and he was practically stepping on his own hair. Red cautioned me quite a bit about my reaction to a dog's first haircut.

"Some people cry," he told me.

"Really?" I asked.

"You'll see," he said.

On grooming day, Jacques went to the Latimer Barber and Beauty Shop. Then Shane made his visit. Last of all, that shaggy ball of fur I called Zeke went downstairs. An hour or so later, he came upstairs a full-fledged poodle. He ran over to me as if seeking shelter from that nasty man who'd cut away his fur.

I picked him up and cuddled him, reassuring him that he was all right. And the tears started rolling down my cheeks. Where was my puppy? I'd sent a puppy downstairs. A dog had returned.

Now I know how my good friend and coworker Rosemary felt when her firstborn child, a son, became potty trained. "I no longer have a baby," she cried on my shoulder that night at work.

Red only groomed for practical reasons, not professionally or for business purposes. I never could convince him to do it for others. He said that cutting our dogs' hair was so time consuming and tedious that it was all he could handle. And he wasn't getting any younger. It also saved us about thirty-five dollars a dog every couple of months.

The dogs knew him and generally trusted him. Jacques Pierre, the patriarch of our clan, was well behaved at grooming time.

"He seemed to know that the better he acted, the quicker he would get out of the sling," Red said.

Shane was the hard one. He squirmed and fought and would get so worked up that often I put an ice cube in a clean washcloth, stood in front of him, and let him lick it. That seemed to calm him. I was there to talk with him and hold his feet.

I usually didn't go downstairs while Red was working. I felt that I would be a distraction to the dogs, but in Shane's case, I was a help.

The behavior of the rest of the dogs at grooming time fell in between Jacques Pierre and Shane.

Maggie could go either way. One time, she would be good, and at another time, she would act up. Jacques Andre was a hard one to trim. He yelped and yipped all of the time Red worked on him. I'd often run downstairs.

"Did you cut him?" I asked, going into that side of the basement.

"No," Red said. "He's acting up again."

"Jacques!" I commanded as I petted him. "Settle down and let Master trim you. He's not hurting you. He wouldn't hurt you."

Putting up with dogs kicking, barking, howling, yipping, and fighting was a lot for Red to handle. He would be so exhausted after a day of trimming that he'd go to bed early. He never painted toenails or put ribbons in their hair as one woman he taught to groom did on her female clients.

When the triplets were little, Star began to develop a bump between her eyes about where the snout began. It was soft and kept getting bigger. It didn't seem to bother her. Red would trim around it. Given my history with a lump, I was concerned. I knew the vet had to see it. How could he miss it?

I mentioned my concern on one visit. He felt around it and got no response from Star. He asked how she reacted to it.

"She acts as though it isn't there," I said.

The vet decided to cut into it. He sprayed an anesthetic on it and made a vertical slit and then a horizontal one. Out came a tan-colored fluid that looked like hand lotion with too much liquid in it. Oh, my gosh! That newly exposed area contained a gob of wet hair. It looked like her hair was growing but could not penetrate her skin. The vet cut the hair and put a little antiseptic on the open wound. We breathed a sigh of relief.

Not long after that, the bump returned. This time, we weren't as concerned or scared. When she made her next visit to the beauty shop, Red cut the bump open, pulled the hair out with tweezers, and put some antiseptic on it. She didn't seem to feel that cut. She never yelped. The bump never grew back.

After grooming, the dogs had a bath. They also had a bath before they went to the vet's office. At times, grooming and baths came right before a trip to the vet.

Red would bathe the dog, using the handheld shower spray in the tub. After the lather and thorough rinsing, he'd try to get the dogs to shake while still in the tub and protected by a shower curtain. Did you ever know a dog to do what you wanted it to do when you wanted it to? He squeezed out as much water as possible before trying to towel dry the dog. Of course, the dog would wait until he or she was out of the tub to shake.

When the dog was towel dried, Red would hand it off to me where I was sitting in the hallway with a beach towel on my lap and my hair dryer at the ready. The dogs loved the warm air from the hair dryer even in the summer. In the winter, we would turn the thermostat a little higher at bath time.

Brushing and combing followed. Their skin was more exposed after a trim and a bath, and I tried to be gentler with the brush. The brushes have fine wire bristles, and I figured that the brush had to hurt their tender skin. I used the brush sparingly at these times, relying more on the comb and the hair dryer.

Their curly hair could get hard to handle if we didn't keep brushing and combing it on a regular basis. It was hard to believe, but each dog had a different texture of hair. Our dogs had tight curls, wavy hair, soft hair, or coarse hair. And five of the dogs were Zeke's offspring.

Keeping the dogs clean as well as frequent brushing and combing helped us keep the flea problem under control. They wore flea collars in the summer when they were at the campgrounds. Running the sweeper about every day also helped lessen the problem that some people have. A flea on a dog meant bath time.

Because poodles don't shed, we eliminated some hair by regular brushing and combing. If we didn't do this regularly, the hair could easily mat. A little hug and a few kind words as I brushed and combed never hurt. I learned to do some brushing with a dog clinging to me and resting its head on my shoulder.

An End and a Beginning

In the late 1980s, Red decided that the middle-management position at the bank was not for him. The budget process was a stumbling block, so he was able to step down and work with the uniformed officers again. By the summer of 1990, he had reached the three-week vacation level, and I also had three weeks from UPI. We had decided to take it all at once and go to Wisconsin.

On Red's last day before vacation, I worked all day at packing food in the refrigerator/freezer and in the pantry, as well as making sure that we had enough clean clothes. Red packed his things when he got home and then took a nap. Red, the dogs, and I were going to leave when I came home from work around midnight on Saturday.

I took a shower, and we finished off what food in the refrigerator we couldn't get in the motor home and started off. After we merged onto the freeway, I stretched out on the couch for a nap. I woke up around breakfast time. We were in Indiana. We passed through Chicago on a Sunday morning around 10:00 a.m.—a good time to miss all of that traffic.

We made it to lower Wisconsin at about supper time. We found a campground—one mainly for hunters and fishermen. After a bite to eat, we went to bed and didn't wake up until dawn. By late afternoon, we were set up in a campground in Door County, that little strip of land that sticks out like a thumb into Lake Michigan. We were ready for a week of exploring. Boat rides. Mosquitoes. Fish boil. Swatting mosquitoes. Wine tasting. More mosquitoes. Musical programs in the state park. Spraying insect repellant. A taste of the Sturgeon Bay food festival. Mosquitoes. Cherry pies. I wouldn't miss those pesky mosquitoes when we moved on.

After a week in Door County, we drove to Oshkosh, where we stayed for three days. We picked a good time to be there. It was right before the Experimental Aircraft Association convention that drew thousands of people. The manager of the campground was putting up markers for extra sites by the time we left. We didn't want to be in the midst of that humongous crowd. We had heard that a million people had attended the previous year when a Russian plane was the featured attraction. That's not a place to be with dogs, especially our small toy poodles.

Our third stop was in Wisconsin Dells. I had been there many years before—the year the first Dionne quintuplet died. What a way to remember things. Red had never been to Wisconsin Dells, and I couldn't remember much myself other than a boat ride around rock formations.

We found many things to do. We took the boat ride to see those rock formations. We left the mosquitoes back at Door County, or else the birds and bats ate all of the bugs in Wisconsin Dells. We took in a country music show with some local entertainers. We weren't too far from Baraboo, so we went to a circus. And who could resist the House on the Rock with an enormous underground museum of collectibles?

We were always back at the campground in time for an evening meal. I took a package of meat from the freezer, put it on a plate, and let it thaw in the microwave during the day. After dinner, Red cleaned the grill, and I washed the dishes. One afternoon in Wisconsin Dells, Red took the dogs on their leashes over to a meadow to run loose. When I finished the kitchen work, I went outside and settled into a lawn chair to read. I glanced up, and running lickety-split across the field toward me was a white poodle.

"That's Maggie," I said, laying the book on my lap as she jumped on me. I picked her up and headed toward the meadow where Red was watching the other dogs.

"Lose a dog?" I asked as I put Maggie on the ground.

"She knew right where to go," Red said.

Toward the end of our stay, we began to feel the strain of being on the road. We still had some food left, since I hadn't counted on eating out a few times. We were always hooked up to water and could take a shower. But somehow it wasn't quite like the shower at home. I would be glad to get home where I had a little more space.

We arrived home about twelve hours earlier than we had planned.

The first thing I did was check the answering machine. I had a message from work.

I knew before we left that UPI was making some changes in the computer system, but I was assured that the change would not hit Columbus until September. I had taken vacation in late July and early August. The message advised me that the computer change had hit Columbus, and I was to be at work on second shift Sunday rather than early Monday morning, my original schedule. That didn't pose any problem for me. The Sunday morning person said that he would stay over to get me acclimated to the new procedure.

That, I soon discovered, was the least of my worries. Moments after I arrived, I learned of wholesale layoffs. Nearly all of the summer help was let go several weeks early. This was the beginning of the end of the wire service as I had known it. We had been through so much in the past several years. Financial troubles. Bounced checks. Being bought by a group of people whom we thought didn't quite understand what we did. Bankruptcy. Being bought by a foreign journalist who didn't speak English. Loss of clients.

Somehow, we had managed to survive the many adversities, but these layoffs began to get close. Another big round of layoffs came in September. We remaining workers hauled out resumes and started cleaning them up. I hadn't seen mine since I started working for UPI in 1968. We all had the idea that this was a lifelong job and that we would each retire from there. The layoffs in October took the person who had joined UPI three months after I did. I really began to get scared.

One morning, when I went to The Ohio State University Hospitals to do a four-hour volunteer shift, I ran into a longtime friend who worked in medical communications. I felt that I knew him well enough to explain everything that was happening at UPI. He said that there was an opening in his department. I told the fellows at work about this opening. I showed them how to do resumes and talked with them about how to handle interviews. None of us had that much experience with resumes. I had gained my experience through Women in Communications when I worked on its job hunt program over the years.

I submitted a resume for the OSU position and was surprised to receive a call for an interview. I even had a second interview. I waited.

UPI faced a 35 percent pay cut vote by the Wire Service Guild—accept the pay cut and stay in business … or reject it and the company becomes a footnote in history. I had dropped out of the Wire Service Guild during the strike in 1974 because I didn't believe in strikes. Therefore, I couldn't vote on the question. Leading up to the vote, I didn't voice an opinion either way. I wanted the company to continue, but I realized that the way it was being run wasn't the way it should have been run. Then there was that part of me that wanted it to end. But if it did, I would be out of work for the first time since I'd graduated from college twenty-five years earlier. It couldn't end.

The day after the vote was announced that the pay cut had been approved, I was offered the position at The Ohio State University Hospital's Department of Communications. I accepted.

I started my new job on December 1. What a difference! I would have an 8:00–5:00 job, five days a week. I was about to find out how the other half lived. But first, I had to get an alarm clock. Working most of my life on a second or third shift, I didn't rely on alarm clocks.

I couldn't rely on the dogs as an alarm clock. I had to get up before daybreak. The dogs didn't want to get up before we did, and I didn't blame them. It was still dark.

I would have to leave the dogs alone for a while, but they wouldn't be alone for long. Red was working a third shift, getting off work at 7:00 a.m. The dogs could crawl back in bed when he did. Zeke liked the bed so well that we often said that if three people lived in this house and each worked a different shift, Zeke would never get out of bed. His favorite spot was under the covers at the foot of the bed. Red worried that he would smother.

Another strange aspect of this new job for me was that I had weekends and holidays off, something I hadn't had since I began working full-time out of college in 1965.

In 1992, Red had worked sixteen years with the bank and chose to retire. That gave him the opportunity to spend much of the summer in a campground, and I divided my time between the two residences: the house and motor home at a campground.

I never dreamed that I would have two homes.

Starting Over

When I started working at OSU, I decided that I needed an exercise program. By working normal office hours, I realized that I could get into a rut of the same old, same old.

Red had always been fitness conscious. He played basketball in high school, was in the army for eighteen months, and then had to work out to meet standards to join the highway patrol. He had to keep fit at that job. He was so regulated to exercise that he kept at it when he started working at the bank. He would run, walk, or ride his bicycle.

My going from an erratic schedule to a normal one provided me with some time to schedule an exercise routine. I immediately purchased an exercise bike and set it up in the bedroom. That solved a few problems. I could watch television or record a program and play it back as I rode the bike. Many times Red and I didn't agree on programs to watch. I even had audio tapes with music designed for different levels of exercise.

Two weeks shy of having had the exercise bike for a year, the pedal fell off. With two weeks left on a warranty, I ordered new pedals. I had started a new rut—that of regular exercise—and I didn't want to stop while I waited for new pedals to arrive.

I remembered the secretary of our department talking about one of her friends who walked every working day at a shopping center near the university campus on her way to work. Since I passed that shopping center, I decided that I would stop there also. I became a regular walker every Monday through Friday morning, starting out with a couple of laps and increasing my distance as I became more comfortable with the routine.

I enjoyed walking. I could go to work at what I still considered unusual hours with a clear head. At times, I walked on my lunch hour. It gave me time to think about projects that I was working on and perhaps how to get over a hurdle.

Working at the hospital gave me time to slip home and check on the dogs or run errands on my lunch hour. I went home a few times. In the summer of 1995, I made several trips home by necessity. Star was approaching thirteen, and her health was failing.

By this time, Red had retired and was spending much of his time at campgrounds. He'd taken a couple of dogs with him in the motor home, and I came home to feed the other dogs and give Star some loving. One day, I knew that she wouldn't make it. I sat on a concrete block beside the big dog cage in the basement and held her on my lap while I read the book *Dog Heaven* by Cynthia Rylant. It was my way of telling the dogs that they could now go to sleep. After I read that book to her, I turned and started up the steps. I was in tears. I called Red on his cell phone at the campground and told him how I felt. He came home, but Star was already gone. She died by herself. She had no human companion with her when she took that last breath. I felt so badly about that. I'm sure that she knew she was loved and had my attention in those waning minutes. I don't know how long she lasted after I read to her.

One afternoon a couple of months later, when I came home from work and let the dogs out the basement door, Misty was excited to see me. She wanted attention more than ever. That was unusual. Between trying to get attention and trying to relieve herself, she collapsed, and I couldn't revive her. I called Red at the campground in Morrow County. When he arrived home an hour later, I relinquished Misty's body to him.

"Maybe we should have paid more attention to them," Red said soberly that day, and he echoed that thought many times afterward.

Was he feeling guilty that he was spending time at the campground with his favorites and leaving the others at home? Was having all of these dogs way too much for us as we aged? By 1995, Red was sixty-seven, and I was fifty-two. He had raised poodles since 1964.

I had tried to spread my love and attention around, but it was hard. Maggie and Jacques were attracted to Red; Pete and Molly were attracted to me. Star and Misty didn't seem to crave attention from one specific person as the others did. It wasn't that we didn't try.

Since Zeke had taken to sitting in my little chair, Red had insisted that Star should have her own chair. He went looking for one, shopping at furniture stores, department stores, and toy stores. My chair that Zeke had taken over was almost as old as I was. Red finally found a chair for Star, a little brown, vinyl rocking chair.

"I didn't want to tell them that I was getting it for a dog," he confessed. "I told them that it was for a child."

Child? Even the grandchildren he had at that time were well past that stage. Star never tried to get onto the rocker. When I put her on the seat, she jumped off quickly. Did the rocking bother her? Or the vinyl surface? None of the other dogs ever tried to get on it or onto Zeke's chair. Red felt rejected because Star didn't like the chair he'd spent so much time looking for. She still played with her "red tockies," which were now past the ragged point and quite stringy.

I bought Misty a special toy. Snuggle fabric softener was then a new product. I liked the word "snuggle." As I was playing with the dogs, I'd burrow my head into their bodies and say "Nuggle." I don't know if they liked it, but I did. At least I didn't get scratched or bitten. Snuggle was offering a hand puppet at the time, so I sent for it specifically to give Misty something to play with. She played with it more than the others did, but not that much. I think I played with it more than anyone else.

Toys were fine for the dogs. We tried a little bit of dog clothing, but I think putting clothes on a pet is overhyped. Red had a couple of little coats for the dogs. Ginger's looked homemade out of pink, fuzzy material that had a strap that went around her belly and fastened to the other side. Jacques Pierre's was a red-and-white knitted one with front legs. I wasn't going to put that coat on Jacques when he went out the back door.

I found a couple of little T-shirts for dogs, one bearing the name "Pierre Cardog," a takeoff on the designer Pierre Cardin. They were cute, but Shane didn't particularly like it, and Zeke outgrew his.

I even crocheted small granny squares to make a coat for Shane, but he didn't like it. They all tried to wiggle out of the clothing like Star did when I tried to keep diapers on her when she was in heat.

I had given up on clothing for the dogs, saying that it was a waste of money. Then Red bought himself a bomber-style leather jacket. Not long afterward, he saw one similar to it for dogs at the shopping center where he had joined me in walking. He had to buy it for Jacques Andre. I had my doubts about it.

I remembered watching Jay Leno and listening to his comments about animals in costume.

"You know your pet wouldn't wear this," he quipped as he showed photos that people had sent him for the Headlines portion of *The Tonight Show*.

Jacques didn't like that jacket. I would put it on him, and he'd stand there. I agree with Jay Leno. Clothes are for humans. They don't belong on dogs. I see photos in newspapers at Halloween of dressed-up dogs and wonder how long those dogs stayed in those costumes.

Dogs don't need clothes. They are born with their own coats.

That Time of Year

Choosing not to neuter the males or spay the females may not have been the best decision we made. We had made it and had to live with it. I had made a mistake once by not paying attention to the females and raised a second litter of pups that we hadn't planned on. We now had four females and three males. At certain times, it posed problems. I guess you could call it "that time of the year," since the females came into heat about once every six months.

It wasn't bad at first with just Zeke and Star. We knew that we were going to breed Star; the only question was when.

She was too young the first time she came into heat. I bought diapers for her, but she wiggled out of them. One night, during her first prime time, Red had gone out of town, and I was left home with the dogs. I kept Star with me in the living room and put Zeke in a back room and closed the door. What howling! I didn't think such a mild-mannered dog could be so noisy. The second time Star came into heat, she was about twenty-one months old, or roughly in her early twenties in dog-to-human years.

Maggie was a little younger—seventeen months—when her litter was born, which would put her in her late teens in dog-to-human years. After my laxness with Maggie, I become more attentive to the females when they came into heat.

We kept them separated as best we could. After Red retired from the bank, it became easier to separate the males from the females at that time. He would take the males to the campground, and I would stay home with the females.

Fortunately, the triplets hit that "time of the year" at the same time. Thank you, Mother Nature! It's about a three-week headache—roughly a week coming in, a week in, and a week going out.

Zeke was eleven when he fathered Maggie's litter, and I didn't know how potent he was after that. Jacques and Pete were questionable. In our dog-raising years, we had five males. Jacques Pierre had two testicles; Zeke had one, and the others didn't show any. I wasn't going to take any chances just because a testicle didn't show.

The few times we faced that problem in winter we used we used the cages from the motor home.

Jacques Andre didn't seem too fazed by the event, but Pete made up for it. He was so attentive; "lovelorn" is what we called it. The girls would be in the cage, and Pete would lie beside the cage. He wouldn't eat much while the girls were in heat, but he sure did chow down after the girls returned to normal.

One time when we faced that situation, I was forced to be creative. We had Maggie and Molly and Pete and Jacques Andre. Red had the males with him at the campground at Springfield, thirty miles away, and I had the girls with me at home. It was okay by Friday to take Maggie to the campground, but it was questionable for Molly. It was Labor Day weekend, and I wanted to go to Rio Grande and Bob Evans Farm for the volkswalks.

By 1993, I had become active with volkswalking. For a couple of years before that, I had been walking every morning at a shopping center on my way to work. I felt that I needed the exercise since it did so much more than burn calories. I could also clear my head with a walk. If I ran into that proverbial brick wall on a project, I could go for a walk, think it over, and find a solution. I also made some new friends.

That fall, we were making plans to go to Fayetteville, West Virginia, for Bridge Day, and I discovered that one thing I could do was a volkswalk—a part of the volkssporting activity that traces its name to its German meaning of "sport of the people." They are noncompetitive, self-paced, inexpensive, and family- and pet-oriented activities where participants do not have to raise money for a cause. I had heard of them and had written a story about them, but I wanted to try my hand—or should I say feet?—at it. I was hooked after that first day. I try to do a volkswalk every week—sometimes two a week or more.

Those Labor Day weekend walks went through the Bob Evans Farm and the town of Rio Grande, close to the Ohio River. I wanted to go. Those walks were a challenge. Not wanting to leave Molly alone all day, I had to devise a way to take her with me.

I put bottles of water in the freezer. I opened our cooler and put it in the freezer. That Saturday morning, I wrapped the bottles of ice in aluminum foil, put them in plastic bags, and stored them in the cold cooler. I also added regular bottles of water. I packed some dog food and a couple of bowls and grabbed my two-compartment backpack. I made sure I had her favorite—Dog Treats, the crispy little tidbits that look like cocktail wieners wrapped in biscuits,

When Molly and I arrived at Rio Grande, I put one bottle of ice in the outer compartment of the backpack and put it on in front of me. Molly went into the compartment closest to me. I had my radio/tape player on, and as I walked through the farm, I sang along to songs on the tape. If I encountered someone on the trail and started talking, Molly would stick her head out of the backpack.

At times she could walk, and I'd take her out and put her on her leash. She walked quite a bit on the town walk. I didn't want her on the ground on the farm and in the woods because I didn't know if ticks were in the area. I knew that she couldn't handle walking the great distance that I did and the ups and downs on the farm. Each of the two walks was a little over six miles.

Between the two walks, Molly had some food and water. On the way home, I put her Dog Treats in a bowl on the floor, and she ate. I'd stop at roadside rest areas and let her have water. She had a great time. She loved the people, and people were surprised that I had a dog with me.

Back home the next morning, I was walking in Bexley on the other side of town. I figured that I could leave Molly at home. I was only going to be gone for about three hours. She had other thoughts. As I gathered up my walking items, she parked herself at the front door.

"You're not going without me," she seemed to say.

I picked up the backpack, found an ice bottle, and took her with me.

Again, she had a good time. I allowed her to walk a little, and we saw a lot of people. She and I went to the campground that evening, where she reunited with the others. I wonder how she told the other dogs of her experiences that weekend … and if they understood.

Pete

Pete got off to a poor start, but with tender loving care, he progressed. He needed that TLC throughout his life, and I tried to give it to him. I loved him. One couldn't help but love the cute little thing. He had that something special about him. It seemed as though he was always smiling; he was a happy little dog.

He was Maggie's second born. Red had delivered—or rather stood by—that morning when the first pup was born.

"I have to go to work," he said as he continued to get dressed. "You have to be the midwife now."

What did I know? I wasn't around when Star's pups were born.

I sat Indian-style on the floor of the bedroom beside the birthing bed—the same light-blue plastic bed with a towel in it—that we'd used for Star. I remembered what our vet had said the last time—seventeen months earlier—about using a towel and not a blanket at birthing time. He had suggested the towel because the blanket we were using was too big. The newborns could get lost in the folds of that heavy blanket.

Maggie curled up on my lap, but when it was time to expel a pup, she got back in the plastic bed. I feared that she couldn't get the pup out herself, and I tried to help. This was Pete. I gingerly reached for his little body and helped guide him along. Maggie made sure that the protective sac was removed. Then she got back on my lap. This was the process through the birth of all four pups—three males and a female. Then she started mothering.

That second-born pup, a male, didn't do well. By the time he was two days old, he was getting cold and not getting enough to eat. We put a little milk in a bowl, heated it for ten seconds in the microwave, and dribbled a drop or two onto his tongue with an eyedropper.

I'd say, "Pete, swallow it." That was the first time I had used the name with him. He liked that milk. He got most of his early nourishment that way. I'd dribble drops of milk on his tongue until he didn't want any more.

At about this time, Misty began exhibiting signs of false pregnancy. Our vet had told us that it was possible that Misty or Molly might exhibit such signs. Nothing had happened with any of the other females throughout the six-week gestation period, and I didn't think anything more about it.

Once the pups arrived, I was concerned that Star might want to take over the mothering aspect, since she had been such a good mother. But neither Star nor Molly showed any interest in the new pups. In their lives, these pups didn't exist. Misty was different. She wanted to be a mother, I guess. I didn't feel safe putting Pete in a cage with her, even though she was giving a little milk. We gave her the female, and she was content. The milk that she provided wasn't enough to sustain the little one, so she would go back to her mother, Maggie, at feeding time.

We fed Pete every couple of hours, and he began to grow and gain strength. Several days later, he was able to get back into the food line with Mama. We figured since he was so small and Jacques was so big that Jacques had pushed him out of the line.

When Pete was a couple of years old, we noticed that he had a slight limp. It was not that noticeable. Red wanted to blame it on mischievous kids in the neighborhood throwing a rock at him, but Pete didn't have any signs of an injury—no broken skin, no lumps, no bruises, no tenderness. I wondered if I had injured him when he was being born.

Then, too, I wondered about his parentage. His father was also his grandfather. Did that have something to do with his limp? He didn't let it bother him. We didn't make a big thing of out it either. If it were his parentage, why weren't the other three dogs affected? We had kept in touch with the family that had adopted the other dogs, and they didn't report any abnormalities. They had been advised of the parentage when they agreed to take the other two pups from that litter.

At that pre-Internet time, I had a Mac computer for what little work I did at home. It had enough memory to type and save. I had read quite a bit about authors sending their manuscripts electronically to their editors. I wondered how it was done. Not only was this beyond my comprehension, it was beyond the capabilities of my computer.

The computers at work were hooked into a mainframe, and we

had access to various files across the company's system. It was different at home. I wasn't hooked up to anything. My computer didn't have much memory. I didn't understand much about technology. My computer wasn't even big enough to handle the Internet when it became popular.

One thing I did have on that computer was a *Wheel of Fortune*-type game that had a little fanfare-type jingle on it. Pete loved that song. He was the only one who recognized it. When I'd be doing some computer work, I'd open that game, and Pete would come running and lie under the chair until I finished. None of the other dogs paid any attention to what was going on. When I realized his attachment to that song, I would go to that game often during my work. I knew that he would be under my chair all of the time I was working. At least I knew where one dog was.

Pete learned quickly that he was my dog. Strange how these dogs knew to whom they belonged. Since Molly was my dog, he allied himself with her. Both were small, but Pete was a little bigger than his aunt Molly. They even knew what cage was theirs when we traveled.

Red teased me about Pete's name. I insisted that his name came from the book and movie *A Man Called Peter*, but after we visited Branson, Missouri, where we attended the outdoor drama presentation of *Shepherd of the Hills,* Red kept telling me that I'd named him from that book. I had never read the book or even heard of it until that trip—with all seven dogs. The story has characters named Maggie, Pete, and Aunt Molly. After seeing the drama, I purchased the book in the gift shop and read it on the way home. Of course, I knew the story, and the reading went quickly.

I'd often seen stories or lists of popular names for dogs. Molly and Maggie often showed up high on the lists. We had chosen some popular names.

Even with seven dogs, I was amazed at how well tempered they were. They all got along well, and only rarely would one snarl at another, even in close quarters in the motor home and at home. Human kids don't get along that well at times.

One problem that we had with Pete was giving him a pill. It was hard to get a pill down this little one.

The dogs were vaccinated every year for distemper, hepatitis, and leptospirosis (DHL). They got a rabies shot every three years and pills to protect them against heartworm. I remember the little white ones they got once a month. Most of the dogs were easy to work with. We'd put the pill in a pair of tongs, put the tongs far back in their throats, and release the pill. Then we'd massage the throats, and they'd swallow it. Then there was uncooperative Pete.

With Pete, we'd go through the procedure—put the pill in the tongs, put the tongs far back in his throat, release the pill, and massage his throat. A few moments later, Pete would cough, and the pill would come up. We'd have to do it again.

At least he wasn't like Star, the other one we had problems with when it came to pill time. When she was pregnant, she loved to get her daily vitamin, because it was big and chewable. But these little white pills were a different story. She seemed to know what was coming, and she'd clamp her mouth shut. It was hard to open her mouth. It took a while, but we'd open her mouth and work the pill down her throat. We tried that old trick of disguising a pill in hamburger or cheese and let the dog eat the nugget of food. It didn't work with Star; she knew what we were doing and would dig out the pill and eat the food.

When we were at the campgrounds, we didn't let the dogs off the leashes, but we could at home.

In 1962, the original owner had an inground swimming pool installed in the backyard. He filled it in when he sold the house. A concrete walkway lined three sides of the pool. About six feet beyond that walkway was a line of evergreen trees. The space behind that had been a garden for a while, but we let it grow into grass, giving the dogs a lot of space to play. To them, it was big, but for city dwellers—or suburbanites, as we are—it was just right. It is a little larger than most backyards in our development. With a fence around it, two gates provide access to the front yard. We kept the gates closed when the dogs were in the backyard.

One day, Red was working in the front yard alongside of the house, and he could see the dogs in the backyard. Suddenly, he felt something rubbing against his leg. He looked down and saw Pete.

"How did you get out?" he asked Pete as he picked him up and carried him to the backyard. "You're an escape artist."

He never did figure out how Pete made it from the backyard to the front yard. At least he knew where to go. I guess that little one needed some companionship at that time.

By late summer of 1996, we were dividing our time among the campgrounds in the Camp Coast to Coast system. We'd spend time at a campground in Morrow County, or at Alum Cove across the road from Alum Creek State Park in Delaware County, or at Tomorrow's Stars at Springfield in Clark County. We were staying in Delaware County when Pete began acting a little sluggish.

He wasn't quite as spry, and I thought that maybe his leg hurt. He lay around the motor home much more than usual.

Oh, no, I thought. *Don't let it be.*

He didn't want to eat. I began to spoon-feed him warm beef broth. He was able to get that down, but I knew that his days were numbered. His lungs had filled with fluid, much like what had affected Shane who had coughed so much in his last few days.

I was distraught, but I didn't want to show it. I was about to lose another dog that had grown close to me. I didn't want to cry in front of Red and the other dogs. I'd get on my bike and ride around the back roads. I had a route of about sixteen miles that I was comfortable riding. I could ride and cry. All I wanted was to ride away my frustrations. Then I'd be back to the motor home to take my turn at nursing the little fellow. This went on for a couple of days before he drew his last breath. Again, I rode that route in tears—tears of grief. We faced a task that we were beginning to dread—digging another grave in the backyard and burying a dog in the late evening.

And then there were three—Maggie, Molly, and Jacques Andre.

Losing Maggie

Fall of 1998 was a time I wish that I could erase from my life.
I had been at The Ohio State University Medical Center in marketing/communications for nearly eight years. I knew that the medical center was experiencing some financial problems. I was writing the weekly staff newsletter *Newsline* and our department had a close line to the chief executive officer. Anything to be communicated to the staff went to our department and to me so that I could put it in the newsletter.

We had been advised that our jobs were secure, but I wasn't feeling all that secure. Several people in our department had started working part-time, mostly the young mothers. Our department experienced a decline in work because some departments had cut back in what they wanted our workers to produce for them, and I wasn't doing all that much. I had been toying with asking if I could go part-time, too, but I didn't have any idea what else I would do or where I could work part-time to make up for the loss in pay. I didn't know what days or hours to propose. I had those thoughts despite what the powers that be had said.

In late October, on a Monday afternoon when my department director asked me to meet her at Human Resources, I had no idea what was going on. I was taken aback when I was told that my position was being abolished. I guess our department was not as secure as I had been led to believe. I accepted it as though I knew it was coming. Maybe I did know it. I asked if I could return the next day to clean my office and give my tasks to other workers. I was assured that I could do that. When I got back to my office that afternoon, I had been knocked out of the computer system as though I had never been there.

Is that one way of saying that I was being fired? I was given one month's pay. Great severance package if I was fired.

I held up on the drive home without as much as one tear. I didn't want to cry or even exhibit evidence of crying because Red and I had plans to go car shopping that evening.

I walked into the house a few minutes later than my normal time and said, "I lost my job today. My position was abolished."

"Are you going to be able to go to look for a car?" he asked as though he didn't hear what I had said.

The car we were looking for was for him, not me, although I could have used a new one too. Now that I didn't have a job, I didn't think that I should buy a new car. I began to wonder why he needed me in the showroom. Was it to back up his selection? I had been with him when he had bought a couple of cars, and generally what I offered was my approval of the color and asked if it would fit into the garage.

I could look at cars, but I knew that I would not be able to make a decision at that time—not like one time when he accompanied me to the dealership to answer my questions, and he found a car that he liked. We came home with two new cars that day.

"I'm fine," I said. I really was fine. I don't think shock had set in.

Red was interested in a particular car, but I didn't see anything that I liked.

"I'm going to have to drive my car a while longer," I said. I was driving Red's Escort, a hand-me-down car.

I was subdued that night, brooding over my situation. Red was quiet, too, but for a different reason.

A couple of days earlier, we'd noticed a little bump on Maggie's belly. She'd had it for quite a while, and it was beginning to grow. We knew what that meant. I don't think we really wanted to talk about it. We discussed it briefly that night—trying to talk about whether a fourteen-year-old dog should have surgery.

If she did have surgery, how could I cope with that along with losing my job? It was the first time since I'd graduated from college in 1965 that I didn't have a job. What was I going to do about getting another at the age of fifty-five? Three times before, I had left jobs voluntarily one day and started a new job the next. Not this time.

I'd had cancer back in 1982. To this day, I don't think that the realization ever set in. I didn't know that I had it. After the surgery, when I was told what was found, I was already set up on a chemotherapy regimen so that it wouldn't return. My idea was that I didn't know I had it, and then when I learned about it, the diseased organs had been removed, and I would be treated to keep the cancer from returning. So I never knew that I had it.

This might have worked for me, but with a dog, I couldn't do things the same way. We decided against surgery because of Maggie's age. She's the one who had clung to her master as though the two of them were attached with a Velcro strip. Now she really needed that human contact. It was good that he was there for her.

Meanwhile, I was doing the modern-day version of pounding the pavement, updating my resume, doing computer searches, and touching base with my network. I still didn't have an Internet-accessible computer at home, so I went to the library a half mile away to do some searching.

I called friends to see if they knew of any job openings. I used my nephew's computer to update my resume that had been created with a program I didn't have on my home computer.

As I worked toward getting a job, I was trying to pay attention to Maggie. The tumor kept growing. And, of course, Molly and Jacques needed my attention. Red was the number-one comfort for Maggie, so someone had to take care of the other two.

It didn't take long to get an interview and then a job. Thank heaven. I could start work on December 1 at Hannah News Service, covering legislative proceedings and state government for a daily newsletter whose clients were lobbyists, legislators, and state government officials. I would get my last paycheck from OSU the end of November, and in the next week or so, I would get a paycheck from Hannah News. My string wasn't broken! I'd had a paycheck for every week or month from the middle of June 1965 on. Not a bad record.

I was even allowed to take a few days off to fulfill an obligation with Mom. She said that she hadn't been in a big plane. She had flown once with us in my small, four-passenger plane. I told her that I'd take her. That summer, I won two tickets on America West. We had decided to fly to Phoenix a week before Christmas for a couple of days. We had a good time and returned to Columbus in time to take Mom to an Ohio State basketball game in the new Schottenstein Center. Ohio State won big. It was a pre-Big Ten season game.

"You call that a basketball game?" asked Mom, who had played in high school and took us kids to games when we were in school.

Maggie's tumor was still growing. She lay in her bed a lot. The tumor was approaching the size of her head. Maggie had a long snout—the biggest of all of our dogs. We always said that you could see Maggie coming because her nose got there a long time before the rest of her body.

Maggie made it through Christmas, although Christmas that year was not as festive as in previous years. I didn't even feel like fixing stockings with dog-food-filled eggs or the wreaths with bones in them. Our concern was all about Maggie. We lost her the day after Christmas 1998. She had turned fourteen in August.

Molly

Molly and Jacques now occupied our time as we entered 1999. When I had been job searching, I found an opening for a sports clerk at the *Columbus Dispatch*. It would be an evening job, four nights a week. I could do the work, no doubt about it. I had done similar work for years at United Press International. I applied. In February, I was called in for an interview.

I made an arrangement with the *Dispatch*. If I didn't write for the paper, I could still write for anyone else. And Hannah didn't care if I worked at night. The Hannah job wasn't a full forty-hour week; it was more like thirty—light on Monday and Friday and busy on Tuesday, Wednesday, and Thursday. The *Dispatch* job was to be not more than nineteen hours a week.

I was now working two jobs, usually from 10:00 a.m. to 5:00 p.m. or so at Hannah, grabbing a salad or sandwich at Wendy's, and then working the *Dispatch* from 6:00 to 11:00 p.m. some nights or from 5:00 to 11:00 p.m. on weekends.

Not long after I started at the *Dispatch*, Molly developed an abscess in her mouth. We had opted against surgery for Jacques Pierre when he developed cataracts and a few months earlier when Maggie's tumor showed up, but we decided on surgery for Molly. Much to my surprise, she came through the surgery with no problems. We were careful about what we gave her to eat and tried to give her soft foods for the first couple of days.

The day after surgery, I thought that we'd try her on some leftover meatloaf. I cut it up in small pieces and put it on a plate. Red held her, and I held the plate. I thought he had a vacuum cleaner in his arms. She inhaled the meatloaf. She was really hungry. How could she even taste it?

She wasn't quite the same after surgery. She wasn't as spry as she once was. And one day, she fell down the stairs. That scared me. I knew that she wasn't going to last much longer. Did that abscess signal something else? I didn't know.

I had to enjoy her as much as I could. She wasn't all that big. She ended up the smallest of the three in the litter. How did I always get the runt? Shane was a runt, Star was small, Molly was little, and so was Pete—and all four picked me.

She had chosen to sleep with me when she was young. Molly didn't curl up beside me like some dogs did. Instead, she slept perpendicular to me—her rear to my stomach. She seemed to be so close to me these days.

About a month after the surgery, the abscess returned, and Red took her back to the vet.

I didn't have to work at the *Dispatch* that evening, so I could have a heavier day than usual at Hannah. I could ride the bus, which stopped about a half block from home, or I could drive my car to the nearby shopping center and leave it in the parking lot and get the bus from there. Since Red retired, much of the work with the dogs fell to him. I had tried to block the day's procedure from my mind so that I could concentrate on my work.

It was dark by the time I arrived home that March evening. Red was waiting for me at the top of the stairs, seven steps up from the front door. His expression told me what I didn't want to hear—that Molly hadn't made it. She'd started hemorrhaging during the surgery and had to be put down.

It was now just him and Jacques and me. He held his arms open, and I clung to him and began to cry as his arms enfolded me.

"I knew she wouldn't make it," I said through my tears. "I didn't think she'd make it through the first one."

I had wanted to be strong and solid, but here I was crying again—and for a dog who had lived fourteen years.

Somehow, I managed to eat something and make it through the evening with one dog. We hadn't been down to one dog for seventeen years. I had to become used to it again.

I knew it wouldn't last long. Jacques was now thirteen.

Then There Was One

We now had just Jacques Andre. He was Red's dog. He liked me all right, but he'd obey Master. Often, I'd try to get him to join me on the couch. I'd call him. Jacques would look at me and then look at Red.

"It's okay, Jacques," Red would say. "You can go to Mistress."

Jacques would look at Red and then at me, and then he would jump up on Red's lap.

"We see where you rate," Red chided.

If I had food, there would be no choice for Jacques, especially if that food was a pretzel rod or a graham cracker. Those were two snack foods he couldn't resist. I could have either in my mouth, and he'd jump up on my lap and munch on the other end.

Since the fall of 1982, we'd had more than one dog in the house. It was strange now. Jacques Andre didn't have the sense his father did when I had lost Shane. I wasn't hurting as much now as I was then. We had different lifestyles now. Red had retired and was spending much of the warm weather in the motor home at campgrounds, most of the time at Springfield about forty minutes from home. I was working about thirty-five hours a week at Hannah News Service downtown covering state government and writing articles for its five-day-a-week newsletter, and I was also working four evenings a week as a sports clerk at the *Columbus Dispatch*.

I was also involved with volkssporting and going somewhere every Saturday morning to walk. In one Saturday event, I could walk six miles and then bike fifteen miles. I put my bike in the back of my red Ford Escort and took off for Yellow Springs, not too far from Springfield. The walk went through the little town, while the biking event covered a part of the Little Miami trail.

"You'll love it," I told Red enthusiastically when I got back. "You don't have to be out on the main roads at all."

He liked to ride a bike but didn't like getting out on the highway. The campground was alongside US Route 40 where Interstate 70 crossed. Traffic was heavy, especially with campgrounds across the road from each other. Even at home, about the only place to ride was on Route 40, which is commonly known as the National Road. That road, which began in 1811 in Cumberland, Maryland, and stretched westward seven hundred miles to Vandalia, Illinois, came through central Ohio in 1833.

He decided that he would try riding his bike on the multipurpose trail.

"I have to go home and mow the yard," he said. "I'll bring my bike back with me."

His bike at that time was about thirty years old. He had bought it in 1970, a yellow AMF three-speed that seemed to weigh a ton.

He went home early Sunday, mowed the yard, put the bike in the back of the car, and returned to the motor home. Late that afternoon, we went out on a segment of the trail not far away. We could bike from there to Yellow Springs, to Xenia, and even to Cincinnati if we were up to it. He made it partway from Springfield to Yellow Springs and begged off, claiming that he was tired.

"After all, I walked behind the mower this morning," was his excuse.

The next Saturday when I got back from a walk, I noticed a red bike in the yard at the motor home. I walked in and looked around.

"Got company?" I asked. "Who belongs to the bike?"

"I bought that for ten dollars this morning from some guy here in the campground who didn't want it," he said.

It was a ten-speed bicycle, allowing him to go faster.

We spent a lot of time on the bike trails in all directions from Xenia. Red now had a ten-speed, and I was plugging away on my three-speed. Other bicyclists were passing us. The next thing I knew, he wanted a better bike. For his birthday, he bought a twenty-seven-speed bike and then took me to the bike store to show me one that he thought I would like. The next time we hit the trail, we were both on new bikes.

Jacques had to stay at the motor home when we went bike riding.

He didn't have any canine companionship. It must have been a lonely life, but I never heard him complain.

In the winter, Jacques kept close to Red at home. The two were always close, and he accepted the fact that I was part of the household. I was the one who often offered him food.

He could hardly wait for spring and getting out in the motor home. He loved it; it was his second home. He and Master were together much of the time.

By August of 2000, he'd started to slow down. I noticed one morning at the motor home that he didn't jump up on the couch like he usually did. Instead, he climbed up on the bonnet, that hood over the motor in the center between the driver's seat and passenger's seat, and then onto the couch. This wasn't Jacques Andre.

I didn't want to admit what was happening. He lay around and didn't want to eat. I feared that we wouldn't have him much longer.

The next day, I fixed a bowl of Frosted Mini-Wheats, a cereal that he liked, and carried the bowl to the couch where Jacques was lying. I wanted to see if he would eat. He hadn't eaten anything the day before. I was overjoyed when he lifted his head and ate some soggy cereal.

"See. He's eating," I said excitedly.

But I could tell from Red's expression that he didn't hold much hope for Jacques. He and Jacques soon rerturned home.

In later years, on August 13, Red would begin to get melancholy.

"This is the anniversary of Jacques's death," he would say in a voice that cracked. "I fed him some broth and put him down here beside the recliner. He took a deep breath, and he was gone."

It had been almost a year and a half with one dog.

Losing a dog was as hard on us as losing a family member. It left a definite void in our lives.

"It's like a tomb around here," Red would often say.

"And how many times did we thank them for letting us share their home?" I asked.

We had to develop a new way of communicating—speaking directly to one another. It was difficult at first. For so long, much of our conversation included the dogs or was directed at them.

For instance, rather than say directly to Red, "Dinner's ready," I would say to the dog nearest me, "Go tell Master that dinner's ready." Not that the dog always obeyed, but the message got through.

Red was a little restless at first and at a loss for something to do. I suggested that he volunteer at an animal shelter.

"I couldn't do that," he said. "I'd want to bring them home."

I could understand that. I'd probably have the same feelings. "Maybe you could take some dog food out, or bathe and groom the dogs," I suggested.

That didn't suit him either. He had tried grooming other dogs before I met him. Some people just don't take care of their dogs as we did, and some of those dogs had hair so matted that it seemed they hadn't been brushed or combed for a year, he said.

He was so meticulous about our dogs. They would have to have baths before going to the vet. Believe me, our vet noticed. I don't know how many times the vet commented on how good our dogs looked.

On a couple of occasions not long after we were married, larger poodles roamed our neighborhood. The dogs didn't have collars and weren't all that friendly, but they hung around our place. We tried to lure them into the garage with dog food.

One stray poodle came in and ate, but we couldn't get it much further. We had more success with the second one who came by. It was a standard poodle and really in need of a bath and a haircut. Red did both. The dog seemed to understand. He got a bath, a haircut, his belly full, and a good night's sleep in the garage. The next morning, Red let the stray outside in the backyard. He jumped the fence for wherever. We never saw him again. In fact, I had never seen him before.

"That's the thanks I get," Red said. "Never again."

He didn't do anything for other dogs for a long time. Long after our own dogs were gone, he accepted a request to dog sit. Our neighbor woman B.J. was going to Las Vegas for a few days and needed someone to watch her dog. We knew CoCo, and CoCo knew us. On occasion, Red would trim CoCo's toenails, but that's as far as he had gone toward caring for another dog.

He was afraid that he'd get too attached to a dog again. He said that it was too hard to lose a dog, and he would have to dig another grave. As he aged, his reasoning against getting another dog changed. "The dog would outlive me."

Concerns about how to handle the grooming also bothered him. His hands were beginning to show the effects of aging. True, the tenderness and caring were still there, but the fingers were not as flexible as they once had been.

Since the only kind of dog that he would have is one that doesn't shed, he feared that I wouldn't be able to handle the grooming. He's right about that. I am too squeamish around the clippers. I am afraid that I'd cut the dogs. I don't think that I could handle their squirming. I don't have the patience. And I think the dogs would know how I felt, and I don't think it would be that easy for me—or them.

Trying to get over losing the dogs was hard. Grief for a dog is as hard as it is for a human. I had trouble coming to grips with my father's illness, hospitalization, and death all in a period of three weeks when I was a junior in high school. But that was forty years earlier. I was all grown up. Or was I?

Being without dogs had its own type of grief. First came the tears … and then the dreams. How do you cope with the dreams? I once dreamed that I held Pete in my arms. I could feel his soft, white, curly hair and feel the warmth of his body. The next thing I knew, I was in the basement beside the dog-run-style cage, now used for storage, looking for Pete.

Pete had been gone a couple of years, but I was looking for him. I remember sitting on the edge of the bed beside Red, his arms around my shoulder.

"Hell, isn't it?" he said solemnly.

"But I could feel the warmth of his body," I cried.

Years later, I still have dog dreams of a white poodle in bed between us … or of opening the back door and seeing three white poodles waiting to be let inside. I dream of Molly sleeping in her usual position, perpendicular to me or of my dogs in need of a haircut.

I wake up scared. I want to go take care of the dogs. When I realize that they are not with us, I almost cry. To answer Red's question of years ago, "Yes, it is hell." I suppose that I'll be haunted throughout my life with dog dreams.

One of the first things that changed after we lost Jacques was the camping. Red no longer enjoyed going in the motor home without a dog.

"It isn't the same," he'd say. He put the motor home in storage.

Without a dog, I could get up in the middle of the night and get a drink of water or go to the bathroom and still have my place in bed. With Maggie having to be so close to Red, she chose to stretch out between us. And Jacques loved a pillow. When I got up, he took over my pillow and lay on it lengthwise.

"You left it, you lost it," Red would say as I tried to get Jacques to move. No success. I learned to go back to sleep without a pillow.

Not having dogs meant that I could leave the house without worry. Many times, when Red and I were working different shifts or when just I would be working, Red would be at the campground with some dogs, and I'd have others at the house. I'd get a mile or so from home and wonder, *Did I let the dogs in?* I'd swing around and return home to check. Yes, they were all okay, safely inside the house.

Would I do it again? Yes, but not on such a large scale. Red maintains that he is too old to care for dogs. "They would outlive me, and what would become of the dogs?" he says.

I'd like another dog, maybe two. I don't think that I could raise one alone. The dog would have to have company. At least that's the way it was when we had dogs. We were both working, and at times, the dogs had to be alone. If we'd had one dog, it would have been lonely.

The life span is in the low- to middle teens, or at least that's what we experienced. Shane was our youngest, and he didn't make it to ten. But then, Red didn't expect him to make it anyway, since he was the runt of the litter and had to be bottle-fed. We had three who made it to fourteen, and that's a long life in dog years.

It took us a long time to get over their losses. Grieving went on for years. A long time. Red was a week shy of his seventy-second birthday when our last dog died. He had had a poodle or two in his life for thirty-six years—half of his life.

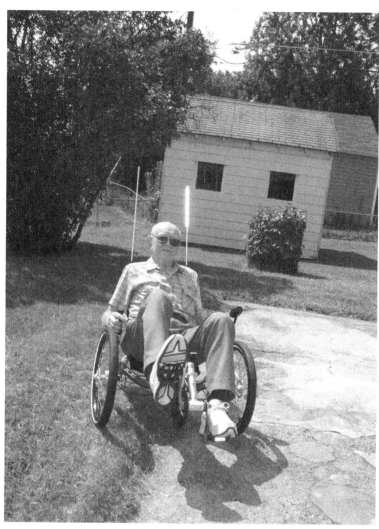

Author's husband Red Latimer tries out his
recumbent trike in summer of 2009

Dogs and Children

We have been without dogs since August of 2000. It's by choice, and we've found it to be about the hardest choice we've ever made. We had decided when Maggie's pups were born in 1986 that those pups would be the last dogs. Red was becoming concerned about his age and whether he would be able to care for them the way that he had taken care of the dogs for many years. We also decided that it was time to do something for us for a change. We had been talking about doing some much-desired repairs at the house.

Our house was built in 1962, and Red bought it in 1973. We had always said that when the last dog was gone, we would do some repairs and painting. We began making lists. Jacques had been gone for five years before any such work was done.

Life was also changing. Early in 2001, I left Hannah and went to work as a reporter for the *Columbus Messenger*, an independent free weekly newspaper that has five editions, one of which circulates in my neighborhood. I was back in newspaper work doing what I really love. I guess I have ink in my veins.

I became more involved in volkssporting and went on weekend walking trips throughout Ohio, and I set up walks in central Ohio. While trying to set up a walking route through Green Lawn Cemetery in Columbus, I stumbled across the opportunity to edit the cemetery's newsletter. A few months later, in the spring of 2003, I was asked to be the volunteer coordinator, working part-time.

We didn't have any dogs, and having something new to work on really took my mind off the loneliness. I still had strong memories of the dogs and their antics, memories as strong as those I had for my father who had passed away some forty years earlier.

I didn't realize how strong grief over the dogs could be or how long it could last. Twenty years after having lost Zeke, I still can't bring myself to make tapioca pudding. I often tell myself that I have to make some, but I can't do it. I open the cupboard door in the kitchen, but I can't bring myself to get the box of tapioca.

Tapioca pudding was Zeke's snack. Once, when I made tapioca pudding, I gave Red the beaters to lick. Zeke jumped up on his lap and started licking from the other side. Every time I made tapioca pudding, I'd put a little bowl of it on the floor for him. He'd come running and push the others out of the way and wouldn't let them have any.

"That dog would kill for tapioca pudding," we say when we talk about making the pudding.

I almost go to tears when I'm in a buffet-style restaurant that has tapioca pudding on the dessert counter.

Zeke also had another strange liking. One morning, Red was having a cup of tea and a cinnamon bun for breakfast. He would dunk the cinnamon bun in his tea. Zeke was in his usual position, sitting patiently, waiting for any tidbit. Red gave him a little piece of bun that had been dipped in tea. Zeke swallowed it without tasting and looked at Red as if he wanted more. Red tried to give him a piece of the roll that had not been dipped in the tea. Zeke wouldn't take it. He had to have it dipped in tea. How persnickety!

Red still eats cinnamon buns today and dips them in his tea. Occasionally, he will mention Zeke's like of the tea-soaked tidbit. To this day, we laugh about that, but we almost cry over tapioca pudding. Are we crazy?

Our dogs were like children to us. Many times when I meet people, they will ask if I have children. "My children were born with four legs and fur," is my reply. Usually, their first response is "You have cats?"

I don't think I look like a cat person. I'm a dog person. I like dogs, and I think dogs sense it. When I'm out walking and approach a person with a dog, the dog will steer toward me and want to jump up on me in a friendly way, seeking a pat on the head. Does my being a dog lover show that much? When I see a dog, I'll say, "Hello, doggie." Then I say to the owner, "I always speak to the dog first." The owners seem to appreciate my preference.

I found a few advantages of having dogs rather than children, but then I didn't have children, so what do I know?

One thing was that I didn't have to buy twenty-eight pairs of Air

Jordan sneakers or fourteen pairs of high-priced denim jeans. We had the usual expenses that people have with children—food and medical bills—but we had one bill that humans don't have: licenses. People don't license their children.

Shopping for food was easy. We bought dog food in twenty-five-pound bags at Sam's Club. We could feed them the same thing every day, and they'd never complain. We'd also buy dog food by the box. Most of them liked Bonz, a piece of dog food that looked like it came from a slab of ham. Some of the dogs had the habit of working the center out of the Bonz and eating that first. It was not unusual to find Bonz treats without centers throughout the living room or basement. Shane thought that they were hockey pucks. He'd bat them across the floor and then chase them.

Molly's favorite was Dog Treats. These look like little pigs in a blanket or cocktail wieners wrapped in a biscuit.

They'd eat canned dog food, too, but after a while, the smell became awful. Could it have been offal?

Our vet visits and bills were tantamount to the pediatrician visits and bills. We'd take them all to the vet at the same time. With two or three, it wasn't bad. I would handle one or two, and Red would handle the other. Often, we'd carry them into the vet's waiting room as a way of protecting them from a sudden attack from another dog—or rather our little ones deciding to go up to a big dog and bark. That's their way of being friendly, but maybe the other dog wouldn't know it.

We always had our dogs on leashes. We could handle two dogs to a leash, specifically by snapping a strap to the collars of two dogs. That strap had a ring where we could hook a leash. I could handle four dogs that way. Red would work with the other three.

The dogs seemed to know where they were going and were quite subdued. It was like they knew where they were going and what was expected of them. Or were they afraid?

They had nothing to be afraid of. Our vet was kind with the dogs. He always told us how well behaved our dogs were and that he could tell that we took good care of them. Of course, they always had a bath right before their visit. We'd try to schedule the visit not long after the haircut. And we always tried to get the first appointment of the day. That way, we didn't have to face the possibility of seeing other dogs in the waiting room. The waiting room wasn't too large, and two people with seven dogs took up a lot of space.

Our vet would pet them and talk with them much in the same way that we did and then pinch some skin at the nape and insert a needle with their vaccines. We never heard a yip out of them.

The first time I accompanied Red to the vet with Jacques Pierre and Shane for shots, Shane slept on the back floor behind my seat all of the way home from Marion. The vet had told us that the shot may affect the dogs in some way. Shane's sleeping was the only time any of our dogs had a side effect from the vaccines.

Vets were considerate, too, with the billing procedures—if you can refer to the bills that way. We were only charged one office call, although we took as many as seven in at a time. I often thought that we should have been given a group discount or a bulk price on the medications, especially when getting heartworm pills.

Our children didn't go to school, and we didn't have a truant officer at the door either. I guess you could say that we homeschooled our brood.

We didn't worry about our kids getting into drugs or alcohol, borrowing the car without asking, or staying out past curfew. We didn't have to pay a babysitter. Only once did Jacques Pierre and Shane stay with someone. That was the fall after Red and I met and were invited to his nephew's graduation at the University of Tennessee. We were traveling with his family and couldn't take dogs. The woman in Marion who had Shane's mother and whom Red had taught to be a dog groomer kept them for the few days we were gone.

With children, someone is left to carry on your name. With no children, no one is there to carry your name into the next generation. You die, and your name dies with you. What do you leave to the next generation? You leave just a lot of memories and a stone with your name on it.

When we lost Jacques Pierre, I kept the ribbon from his flowers. I bought yellow roses for Shane and Zeke and kept the yellow ribbons after the flowers died. I taped the ribbons to a photo of those three dogs, which hung in the living room until the summer of 2006 when we painted the walls and put down fresh carpeting. The photo went back on the wall, but the ribbons went into a box of dog-related items in the closet in the back room.

Nine dogs are buried in the backyard near what used to be a flower bed. Grass has grown over those graves, but memories linger.

Epilogue

Early in our marriage, my stepdad gave us a squirrel feeder for Christmas. It was a wooden ledge with a long nail to put an ear of corn on. Red put it out on the redwood fence in the backyard. Occasionally, we'd locate an ear of corn.

I never really liked that fence. It was put up as a privacy fence by the original owner who had a swimming pool. The pool was filled in to make the house easier to sell, but the fence remained. Several years later, it became an eyesore, was dilapidated, and didn't add anything to the backyard. We tore it down. The squirrel feeder found a new location on one of the trees in the front yard. It was easier to see. We found ears of corn near the campgrounds and started spiking them regularly. If you feed squirrels, they will come. They came. We watched.

Meanwhile, I heard about squirrel houses and talked to several people about them. I found the directions on how to build them through the Ohio Department of Natural Resources and brought them home. Red looked at them.

"I'm not a carpenter," he said and filed the directions away.

One day, about four years after losing Jacques Andre, I heard pounding in the basement and went down to check it out. Red is a country boy; he grew up on a farm in northwest Ohio and went to high school during World War II. At that time, boys took shop and made toolboxes; girls took home economics and learned to cook and sew. No one crossed the line.

After high school, he served eighteen months in the army—between World War II and the Korean conflict. Although he spent much of his hitch in Korea, he is still considered a World War II veteran. He used his GI bill money to go to plumbing school, and he worked as an apprentice electrician until he turned twenty-three and could join the highway patrol. No wonder he says that he isn't a carpenter.

Pounding? He was making a squirrel house to hang on the tree above the feeder.

"Freddie and Freda have to have a place to live," he said.

"Freddie and Freda?" I questioned.

"Yeah, the squirrels."

"Okay," I said and went back upstairs. "Now he's naming the squirrels. I guess since we don't have dogs, he has to have something to do."

He put the squirrel house on a tree in the front yard and watched it carefully, day by day.

"A squirrel went in the house," he yelled one morning, running down the hallway.

We watched for quite a while. Soon, a squirrel came out and sat on the ledge.

"See, they're using it," he said excitedly. "Now Freda will have some place to have her puppies."

"Puppies?" I asked. "Squirrels don't have puppies."

"They do here," he said.

That sent me to the computer to start looking for information on squirrels. What do you call the baby squirrels? The only thing I could find was "infants."

We gleaned cornfields after the fall harvest and filled dog food bags with corn for the squirrels. When we stopped camping and ran out of ear corn, we bought bags of shelled corn at the Tractor Supply Company/TSC store down the street. Squirrels would come and go, come and play, come and eat. One time, I counted ten squirrels playing on the tree, scurrying in and out of their house just like kids—or even monkeys. What a laugh we got out of them that day.

"I want to see babies," Red would say.

In the spring, he got his wish. Three babies.

I would buy peanuts, toss out a few out on the front step, and watch the squirrels come running.

"Hey, you have a friend out here sitting up for peanuts," Red called to me one day.

I dropped what I was doing, grabbed a handful of peanuts, slowly opened the front door, and tossed the peanuts toward the squirrel.

For twenty-seven years, I babied poodles. Now I'm babying squirrels.

The Latimer Poodle Family

Jacques Pierre	May 22, 1965–September 13, 1977
Shane Andre	May 17, 1973–August 11, 1982
Ezekiel Jacques Pierre "Zeke"	December 10, 1974–August 14, 1989
Lady Bell Star "Star"	September 4, 1982–July 20, 1995
Molly Bee	August 1, 1984–March 18, 1999
Maggie Belle	August 1, 1984–December 26, 1998
Misty Star	August 1, 1984–October 22, 1995
Peter John "Pete"	January 21, 1986–September 2, 1996
Jacques Andre	January 21, 1986–August 13, 2000

Acknowledgments

If it hadn't been for my boss, John Kady, scheduling me to work that night in July 1973, I would never have met a gentleman who raised toy poodles. I married this man, Hugh "Red" Latimer, several months later and became known as Mistress to these little ones.

Red understood my love of writing and at one time encouraged me to write something about each of the dogs. More than twenty-five years later, I finally started putting words to paper about our lives with the dogs.

My colleagues and friends in Ohio Professional Writers, Ohio Writers Guild, Writers' Ink, and NFPW listened to and read my work, offering guidance and assistance in editing and revising as well as the much-needed encouragement. Although I had edited and proofread newspaper articles for many years, I learned a lot from these patient people.

I'm so grateful for the coffee breaks and lunches that I shared with my friend Judith Rogers as she helped me bring my words into the form you have just read, as well as the support she provided for me every step of the way.

Although writing has been my calling for many years, the task of wiring a book has been a new experience, and I have enjoyed every minute of it.

My newfound writing style goes on. I try to take time from work or volunteering to write something every day.

Although Sandi Latimer was born in Columbus, Ohio, she grew up in the rural, north central Ohio area of Crawford County. Her writing career began in eighth grade with a job at her local newspaper. After graduating from Kent State University with a degree in broadcast journalism, her writing expanded. She has worked in broadcasting, public relations, and newspapers, but most of her writing came during her more than twenty-two years at United Press International in Columbus. It wasn't until she was married and "Mistress" to the dogs that her thoughts turned to creative writing. Years later, as she turned to part-time employment, she began to write creatively, with adventures with the dogs as her first effort. She and her husband, Red, still live in Columbus, and the motor home is in storage.

CPSIA information can be obtained
at www.ICGtesting.com
Printed in the USA
FSOW03n2256100117
29471FS